Letts **explo**

The

Arthur Miller

Guide written by John Mahoney

A *Letts* Literature Guide for GCSE

Contents

Plot summary

1 Act 1: Salem 1692. Reverend Samuel Parris worries about his daughter Betty, who has been lying, unresponsive, since he discovered her dancing in the woods with his niece Abigail and friends – a forbidden activity for Puritans.

4 John Proctor, a local farmer, comes to find his servant, Mary. He talks alone with Abigail, his one-time serving girl, with whom he has had an affair. She wants to pursue the relationship, but he does not.

2 Parris questions Abigail about the girls' activities, since many are now ill for no obvious reason. Witchcraft is suspected, particularly by the Putnams, whose daughter Ruth is affected. Parris has sent for the Reverend Hale, an expert. Abigail denies that anything of a devilish nature has taken place.

3 Abigail instructs Mercy Lewis, Mary Warren and Betty on what line they will take and what they will admit to. It is clear that though they have been dabbling in spells, none of them is really bewitched.

12 John denounces Abby as a whore and admits to adultery. He asks the court to question Elizabeth on this matter, believing that she is incapable of lying. Not knowing of his confession, Elizabeth denies John's guilt and so saves Abby and condemns her husband.

11 Mary Warren says that all the girls are pretending. The girls maintain that Mary is bewitching them.

15 Reverend Parris is frightened about the repercussions of hanging respected citizens, like Goody Nurse, and tries unsuccessfully to get the deaths postponed. Abigail and Mercy Lewis have run away.

13 A hysterical Mary, frightened by the other girls, accuses John of being the devil's man. Horrified by what is being allowed to go on, Hale quits the proceedings.

14 Act 4: Hale has returned to Salem to pray with the condemned prisoners; he wants all to be pardoned.

5 Hale arrives and starts his investigation. Abigail implicates Tituba, Parris's servant. When Tituba reveals names of women who she has seen with the devil the girls hysterically join in.

7 Hale visits the Proctors. He is disturbed by John's poor attendance at church and inability to recite all Ten Commandments. John tells him about Abigail's lies to the court.

6 Act 2: Elizabeth Proctor urges John to go to Salem to denounce Abigail as a fraud, since so many are being accused of witchcraft. Their servant Mary returns from court and gives Elizabeth a doll she has made.

8 Giles Corey and Francis Nurse appear with the news that their wives have been arrested, and then officials come to take Elizabeth, who has been accused by Abigail. Mary's doll forms the main proof of witchcraft.

John is suspected of trying to undermine the court because he will not drop the charges against others, even though his wife, who has just announced her pregnancy, is to be spared from hanging for a year.

9 Act 3: Giles Corey and Francis Nurse try to expose the lies in court to Judge Hathorne and Deputy Governor Danforth.

16 To save him from being hanged, Elizabeth is asked to try to get John to confess. She tells John that Giles has died courageously, being pressed under rocks.

17 John decides to make a false confession, which horrifies Rebecca Nurse, who is about to be hanged. He refuses to implicate others.

18 John rips up his signed confession, not wanting this lie publicly displayed. He goes to his death, acknowledged by Elizabeth and Rebecca as a good man.

Who's who in *The Crucible*

John Proctor

John Proctor is the <u>central</u> <u>character</u> of the play and husband to Elizabeth. He is a farmer in his middle thirties, respected by the town's people. He has a 'quiet confidence' and a 'hidden force'. <u>The</u> <u>focus</u> <u>of</u> <u>attention</u> <u>is</u> <u>on</u> <u>his</u> <u>moral</u> <u>choice</u>. Arthur Miller wrote that he was drawn to the image of 'a guilt-ridden man ... who, having slept with his teenage servant girl, watches with horror as she ... points her accusing finger at the wife he has himself betrayed'.

John Proctor is a strong character, '<u>powerful</u> <u>of</u> <u>body,</u> <u>even-tempered</u> <u>and</u> <u>not</u> <u>easily</u> <u>led</u>', whose guilt makes him indecisive until it is too late. In some ways he is a <u>typical</u> <u>tragic</u> <u>hero</u> – a good, honest man with a secret, <u>fatal</u> <u>flaw</u>. A <u>natural</u> <u>leader</u>, he has the ability to organise opposition to the court. John Proctor is <u>independent-minded</u> and a <u>good</u> <u>Christian</u> who allows his church-going to be affected by his distaste for the greed and selfishness of Parris. He is an <u>honest</u> man who is undermined by his one act of dishonesty: betraying his wife and concealing his guilt. He is obviously a passionate man and he <u>sees</u> <u>himself</u> <u>as</u> <u>a</u> <u>sinner,</u> unworthy to follow in the footsteps of such martyrs as Rebecca and Giles. Finally, however, he realises that he cannot betray the others and still keep his integrity, <u>so</u> <u>he</u> <u>welcomes</u> <u>the</u> <u>marvel</u> <u>that</u> <u>he</u> <u>has</u> <u>found</u> <u>some</u> <u>goodness</u> <u>in</u> <u>himself</u>.

Elizabeth Proctor

Elizabeth Proctor, John's wife, has unshakeable <u>religious</u> <u>belief</u>, but she also loves and feels strong <u>loyalty</u> <u>for</u> <u>her</u> <u>husband</u>. She, too, faces a <u>moral</u> <u>dilemma</u> during the play. She is a good wife in the traditional sense, but during the first half of the play there is a strong sense of the 'separation' between herself and her husband. Under questioning, her <u>calmness</u> and <u>integrity</u> are apparent, and so the audience is surprised that she <u>goes</u> <u>against</u> <u>her</u> <u>religious</u> <u>principles</u> and tells a lie when she thinks it will save her husband. Tragically, it has the opposite effect.

Although Elizabeth struggles with her husband's infidelity during the play, she is finally able to <u>forgive</u> him his adultery. When she is arrested, her first thought is for her children. Both John and Abigail accuse Elizabeth of <u>coldness</u>, and, in a moment of self-realisation, she later admits this herself. Early in Act 2 her behaviour shows reserve and an edgy restraint, yet at the end of the play she shows compassionate and clear-sighted understanding of John's dilemma. She understands that if he confesses he will not be able to live with himself. She therefore does not put pressure on him to confess, and <u>puts</u> <u>his</u> <u>spiritual</u> <u>well-being</u> <u>before</u> <u>her</u> <u>own</u> <u>desire</u> <u>for</u> <u>him</u> <u>to</u> <u>live</u>.

Abigail Williams

Orphaned niece of Reverend Parris and previously a servant in the Proctor household, Abigail is a key figure whose activities are crucial to the development of the play. On her first entrance she is described as having 'an <u>endless</u> <u>capacity</u> <u>for</u> <u>dissembling</u>' (pretending or deceiving), so nothing she says or does is to be trusted. Her <u>sexuality</u> and <u>charisma</u> are key influences on Proctor and others, and her actions in the woods – drinking blood and dancing naked – reveal her earthy and dangerous sexuality. Her dismissal from the Proctors' and subsequent failure to find work have left her <u>embittered</u> and <u>determined</u> <u>to</u> <u>pursue</u> <u>her</u> <u>own</u> <u>interests</u> <u>at</u> <u>all</u> <u>costs</u>.

We learn from her exchanges with John that Abigail is still obsessed by him and dreams of being with him. She is extremely <u>jealous</u> <u>of</u> <u>Elizabeth</u> and uses her power to rid herself of John's wife and anyone else who may have insulted her in the past. With her strong personality and well-judged threats, she easily manipulates the other girls, and her exchanges with Danforth show her arrogance and quick-witted cunning as she quickly abandons one strategy in favour of another.

Abigail is in many ways the opposite of Elizabeth: she is worldly, opportunistic, vain, passionate and dominating – everything that Elizabeth is not. She is ambitious and has a clear lust for power, which she achieves when she is given a full hearing by the trials. Suddenly she finds she can control the destinies of others, when previously she had been shunned for her suspected adulterous and wanton behaviour. The fact that she disappears from Salem with Mercy and Reverend Parris's money, leaving the chaos of the witch-hunt behind her, after effectively causing the deaths of nineteen innocent people, illustrates her total lack of morality or concern for others.

Reverend Hale

Reverend John Hale, a 'tight-skinned, eager-eyed intellectual', is the first outsider to hear of the 'witchcraft' and thus a primary cause of the trials. By the end, however, his opposition to the executions is fervent and agonised. He arrives eagerly and full of confidence, a supposed 'expert' on witchcraft: his books are 'weighted with authority' and he believes unshakeably that his expertise will solve the problem. However, his confidence is eroded when he realises that human beings do not act according to the rules.

He naively attempts to convince the condemned to admit to witchcraft in order to save themselves, which he sees as preferable to dying. Hale sees the injustice being done, yet he is willing to go along with the will of the people in order to protect himself. By the time he changes his ways at the end of the play, it is far too late for him to have any influence. This failure results in a once confident man being broken – he sacrifices his belief in both witchcraft and the law. By Act 4, as an audience <u>we</u> <u>regard</u> <u>him</u> <u>with</u> <u>some</u> <u>sympathy</u>, but <u>we</u> <u>cannot</u> <u>respect</u> him because of his lack of moral courage.

Reverend Parris

Reverend Samuel Parris, Betty's father and Abigail's uncle, is <u>a</u> <u>striking</u> <u>contrast</u> <u>to</u> <u>Reverend</u> <u>Hale</u>. He is <u>materialistic</u> and his <u>self-interest</u> has divided the village (he has demanded more money and possessions, even preaching from the pulpit in order to achieve this). He spent some years as a merchant in Barbados, which might explain his regard for wealth and social position. He is <u>proud</u> <u>yet</u> <u>cowardly</u>, resenting insults but fearing anything that might undermine his position. At the start of the play, he is terrified of the consequences for himself of his daughter's and niece's actions, fearing that the community will see that he cannot even control what happens under his own roof. Because of this, he is <u>only</u> <u>too</u> <u>happy</u> <u>to</u> <u>apportion</u> <u>blame</u> <u>elsewhere</u>.

Danforth

Deputy Governor Danforth, a 'grave man in his sixties', represents the <u>combined</u> <u>authority</u> <u>of</u> <u>church</u> <u>and</u> <u>state</u> in this theocratic society. In the face of conflicting and dubious evidence, his is not an easy job, yet he does nothing to stop the court proceedings. Danforth, in fact, is a striking picture of a man of intelligence and apparent humanity who refuses to admit possibilities outside the strict confines of his, or his Church's, version of truth. He feels contempt for many of the foolish witch-hunters; he seems to understand people, but <u>he</u> <u>applies</u> <u>the</u> <u>law</u> <u>with</u> <u>a</u> <u>rigid</u> <u>and</u> <u>unbending</u> <u>harshness</u>. His character makes him unable to believe that the events might be caused by deception, rather than real evil. Certainly, he is unwilling to see his authority flouted. Miller believed that Danforth was the real villain of the play, and regretted that he did not make him seem evil enough.

Mary Warren and the other girls

Mary is the Proctors' serving-girl. She is timid, 'a mouse', easily influenced and hysterical. She enjoys her brief authority in court without really understanding what is going on, but becomes the key witness in John Proctor's accusation against Abigail. She is too weak to withstand the influence of the strong characters, John and Abigail, and has little concept of truth or principle. The other girls have few individual characteristics, though ironically, Mercy Lewis emerges as sly and malevolent. However, as a group, they make a vital contribution to the play. It is essential that the audience believes in the power of hysteria, and their joint actions make the climax to Act 3 very chilling.

Giles Corey and Rebecca Nurse

These characters represent the innocent victims in Salem, whose consciences will not allow them to confess to something they did not do. The moral strength of Giles in refusing to give in to dreadful torture after inadvertently causing his own wife's death, and Rebecca's patient acceptance of her fate, are examples of moral integrity for John.

Mr and Mrs Putnam

The Putnams exemplify the narrow-mindedness and misapplied religious fervour of the community. They are superstitious and bitter about their personal misfortune, greedy in business dealings, envious and small-minded, although, hypocritically, not above seeking information from the black arts with the help of Tituba.

Tituba

Tituba, Parris's black slave from Barbados, is responsible for the start of the witch trials. She is clearly guilty of a tribal, voodoo-like witchcraft, yet she is <u>innocent</u> <u>of</u> <u>evil</u> <u>intent</u>. To her, the devil is a 'pleasureman'; sadly she is in the wrong place. She has acted irresponsibly, no doubt at the instigation of the girls, and perhaps she enjoyed her brief moment in the spotlight when they actively sought out her company. Her concern for Betty is obvious. She is <u>out</u> <u>of</u> <u>place</u> in the strict, cold principles of Massachusetts and is very much a subservient outsider.

Arthur Miller

'The theater is so endlessly fascinating because it's so accidental. It's so much like life.'

(Arthur Miller)

Arthur Miller, who was born into a Jewish family in New York in 1915, is a first-generation American, his father having emigrated from Austria as a child. The family became short of money in the years of the Great Depression and although Miller wanted to go to university, he did not have the finances – or the grades – to achieve this straight after school. As a result, he took on diverse jobs, ranging from warehouse clerk to truck driver.

Miller has said that he read nothing as a boy, his only interest being football, but by chance he picked up a weighty Russian novel, Dostoyevsky's *The Brothers Karamazov*, which he read on the train to work. This directly influenced him to become a writer. He saved most of his salary and persuaded the University of Michigan to accept him on a journalism course. He began writing then, and even won first prize in a competition with a play he had completed in six days, which enabled him to change to an English course. He had his first stage success in 1945, achieving a short run on Broadway.

By this time, his experiences in the Depression years and his awareness of the horror of Fascism in Europe had led him towards Communism. Although he was no longer a member of the Communist party, Miller still held left-wing views. These views are apparent throughout the great quartet of plays that made his reputation and set new standards for American realist drama. As well as displaying sympathy towards 'ordinary' people, these plays, all of which have tragic impact, dwell on the need for personal integrity.

Apart from *The Crucible* (1953), Miller's most famous plays are set in America in the 1940s and 1950s. All share a concern with the problems of personal choice. *All My Sons* (1947) searches the conscience of an industrialist who has caused the deaths of American airmen in World War Two by supplying faulty parts. *Death of a Salesman* (1949) explores the broken world of an ageing salesman whose dreams are shattered. *A View from the Bridge* (1956), is about the betrayal, in a fit of jealousy, of illegal Sicilian immigrants by their Italian-American host. Despite much success since then, these four plays remain Arthur Miller's supreme achievement, and *The Crucible* takes its place among them as the only one which uses a historical perspective to attack the failings of the USA in the immediate postwar years. Apart from the play's political implications, it is thought that it has a very personal slant, with Miller, who had marriage difficulties at the time of writing, identifying closely with the character of John Proctor. He dedicated the play to his wife, Mary, but left her soon afterwards.

Apart from his plays, many for radio, Miller's output includes novels, short stories, a volume of autobiography, *Timebends* (1987), and books of reportage in collaboration with his third wife, Inge Morath, a professional photographer. He has also produced film scripts, including *The Misfits* for his second wife, the film star Marilyn Monroe, and the adaptation of his own work for the film version of *The Crucible* (1996). Although *The Crucible* was received far more enthusiastically by European audiences than by American ones in the early years, it remains Miller's most performed play. Miller has commented that one reason for it being a failure as 'commercial entertainment' was because 'Nobody knew what a crucible was'.

For a chronology of Miller's life and work visit:
http://www.ibiblio.org/miller/life.html

Arthur Miller has written that he wants theatre audiences 'to heighten their awareness of what living in our time involves'. He achieves this in *The Crucible* (1953) by studying the mass hysteria of Salem in 1692 in order to comment on events in 1950s America. Miller is interested in *causation* – how the past contributes to the present predicament.

What happened in Salem in 1692?

The coastal settlement of Salem, Massachusetts was developed some years after the arrival of the Pilgrim Fathers in 1620. In 1692, therefore, the area was still somewhat unsettled. The people led a tough life, fraught with many dangers. Their strict Puritan religion dictated every aspect of the way they lived. They were ruled by a theocracy – a form of government operated largely by the church. To exist under such close control meant that any deviation from the norm could prove very subversive, as the events in Salem proved. These people were highly superstitious and believed strongly in the Devil, which partly explains why the idea of witchcraft, once suggested, took such a hold.

Salem was a divided society, and problems were exacerbated by disputes over the contract of the minister, Reverend Samuel Parris, whose daughter, niece and friends formed a fortune-telling circle with the slave, Tituba. Their alarming experiences quickly led to unstable behaviour and they were mistakenly diagnosed as being bewitched. Any actions against God rocked the foundations of this society, hence the urgent need to discover all perpetrators of witchcraft. This led to mass hysteria and to matters getting completely out of hand, resulting in the imprisonment of hundreds and the hanging of 19 people and two dogs.

As Miller writes in his Preface, 'the play is not history in the sense in which the word is used by the academic historian'. He has maintained the 'essential nature' of the episode, while modifying full historical accuracy for dramatic purposes, as have almost all playwrights of historical drama from Shakespeare onwards.

What happened in the USA, 1950–56?

In *The Crucible in History and other Essays*, Miller looks back to the 1950s and reveals his thinking and sense of personal danger at a time when America was permeated by paranoia and suspicion, fearing Russian influence and control during the Cold War. This was the time of McCarthyism, named after Senator Joseph McCarthy, who claimed that he had a list of 205 people in the State Department were known to be members of the American Communist Party, some of whom were believed to be actively undermining the US government. Working in conjunction with the FBI, over the next few years McCarthy and HUAC (the House UnAmerican Activities Committee) investigated numerous people, particularly in the entertainment industry. Many lost their jobs in this witch-hunt. The only way that they could guarantee safety was – as in *The Crucible* – to name other people. Miller himself was questioned, but not until 1956 when the hysteria was dying down. Like John Proctor, he refused to implicate others, but luckily escaped punishment.

A National Theatre production of *The Crucible*

Themes and images

Conscience

Several characters in the play face dilemmas of conscience. The duty to follow one's conscience has to withstand the desire to preserve one's good name, freedom and even life. Some characters, like Parris and Danforth, would say that it is not the duty of good Christians to follow their individual consciences, but to obey the rulings of the Church. The conflict between conscience and obedience plunges the town of Salem into tragedy. It is only when tragedy strikes at his family directly that Proctor starts to struggle to come to terms with his duty – unfortunately, too late for his family and his community.

Although John Proctor's decision is central to the drama, others, notably Hale and Elizabeth, have difficult choices too. John is faced with complex moral dilemmas several times in the play and, as it unfolds, we see his spiritual development, courage and integrity. Rebecca Nurse and Giles Corey have no difficulty in bravely following their consciences, while Abigail appears to have little conscience about the tragic results of her lies.

Evil

An atmosphere of evil permeates the play. It can be seen in Abigail's pretence, Mercy's slyness, the self-centredness of Parris, and the Putnams' mean and avaricious view of life. The zeal with which 'witches' are hunted and persecuted is a manifestation of evil. The play also contains the trappings of witchcraft – the drinking of chicken's blood, a toad in the kettle and the use of dolls to inflict harm on others. This is black, devilish magic, giving rise to Abigail's 'marvellous cool plot to murder'. Evil gathers momentum, with the people of Salem soon falling into the trap of manipulating others for their own gain or self-preservation.

Identity

Identity comes to the fore in the dramatic turning point when John rips up his confession because signing it will be signing away his name, his very self. His name is more than a courtesy title, like 'Mister', for it defines who he is and links to respect and reputation. Without his sense of identity he cannot live. Elsewhere in the play the idea of reputation is again linked to name. Parris is concerned about whether Abigail's name is 'entirely white', for if it is not it will compromise his character and reputation. Hale has heard Rebecca's name, linked with good works, before he arrives in Salem, but this is not enough to save her from the gallows.

Society

The Puritan society of Salem was bound by strict codes of behaviour and belief, where the word of the Bible was slavishly followed and where stepping out of line in any way could lead to suspicion and accusation. On the surface society was united, but the cracks were there, apparent in the arguments and the high turnover of three ministers in seven years. The 'rules' covered a mass of jealousies and grievances, which took the witchcraft hysteria as an opportunity to burst out. Indeed, the girls' hysteria developed precisely because of the restraints of their society: they feared being shamed and punished for their forbidden activities in the wood. To avoid persecution – something for which the Puritans originally fled England – they persecuted others. The extent to which their society had become divided is indicated by the strength with which general persecution took hold. Many felt it was safer to join in than to stand up for their beliefs.

There was no room in Puritan Salem to act as an individual. In the play, when John wants to speak as he feels, Parris is horrified at any sort of individual expression (such as that which Quakers encourage) because he sees it as undermining the authority that binds society together. Initially, a common set of beliefs had helped people to conquer a difficult environment in a new land. Now that the community was fairly well established, as Miller points out in the introduction, the balance was beginning to turn towards the possibility of greater individual freedom, and witchcraft was a 'perverse manifestation' of the panic arising from this. The extent of society's collapse is shown in the play through the images of homeless children, untended crops and abandoned cattle. Sadly, it takes the deaths of John, Giles and Rebecca to initiate its rebuilding.

Vengeance

Vengeance – the inflicting of punishment or taking of retribution for a perceived injury or wrong – is a pervasive theme in the play. It provides the motivation for many Salem inhabitants, who use the witchcraft hysteria as an opportunity to settle grudges, whether it be to gain land (the Putnams) or possibly marriage (Abigail). It comes to represent a great power, as shown in the personification in Proctor's words: 'Vengeance is walking Salem'.

Fear

The witch-hunt is both caused and fuelled by fear. Of all the characters, only Rebecca Nurse and Giles Corey seem unafraid. The hysteria generated by the girls, stemming from their fear of being punished for dancing in the forest, creates an atmosphere in which fear becomes the motivating force. Fear of being accused leads neighbour to accuse neighbour. Parris's fear of losing his position as Salem's minister leads him to join the witch-hunt. John Proctor's fear that his adultery will be made public means that he delays discrediting Abigail. Mary Warren's fear of Abigail makes her withdraw her accusations and accuse John Proctor instead. Elizabeth's fear for her husband's good name leads her to lie and therefore destroy his evidence against Abigail.

The crucible

A crucible is literally a heatproof container in which substances may be melted or subjected to very high temperatures, which can cause any impurities to rise to the surface. Metaphorically it means a place of severe test or trial. Although the metaphorical use is the one which Miller intends, he shows us two literal and contrasting 'heatproof containers': the kettle – a sort of witches' cauldron – and Elizabeth's pot of stew. Images of heat and cold run through the text, ranging from John's lust for Abigail (heat) to Elizabeth's role as a wife (cold). Salem becomes a crucible, where passionate, heated feelings reign and Danforth burns 'a hot fire' to try to force the supposed witches to the surface and to purify Salem. Miller tried out numerous titles before settling on this one only four weeks before the first Broadway run.

Light and dark

The motif of light and dark runs through the play to signify the theme of good versus evil. In the 1996 film version, Danforth is seen snuffing out a candle as he excommunicates John Proctor and Rebecca Nurse, symbolising the darkness taking over Salem. John can see no 'light of God' in the minister Parris, who barely mentions God in his services, and Putnam thinks that there is a murdering witch among them, 'bound to keep herself in the dark'. In the introduction, Miller writes that the Puritans believed that 'they had in their steady hand the candle that would light the world'. Certainly Danforth feels that light is returning to dusky Salem through the justice of the court, failing to understand the dark deception at the heart of the trials. True light, goodness and hope only begin to emerge as a result of John's noble death. Miller also uses light and dark pointedly in the stage directions, particularly during the final moments of Act 4.

Text commentary

Act 1 (an overture)

The essays that appear in this Act were added in 1958 to set the scene and give background information. They are **delivered** **on** **stage** **by** **an** **actor** **cast** **as** **'The** **Reader'**, but most modern productions omit them.

> **"spring of the year 1692"**

Spring is traditionally associated with **re-birth**. Sunlight, which promotes **growth**, streams through the window. It is ironic that spring and sunlight here **foreshadow** **darker** **events**. The atmosphere of this first Act, set in a small upstairs room in Parris's house, is **claustrophobic**. The smallness of the room and the 'narrow window' symbolise the narrow-mindedness of the community and, as the setting for the different emotions let loose, help to intensify their effect.

This **scene** **is** **charged** **with** **fear,** **guilt,** **hate** **and** **envy**. There is a series of exits and entrances as all the main characters, except Danforth and Elizabeth, are introduced. This creates a sense of activity and introduces the title image of **the** **crucible** **or** **melting-pot**, in which basic elements are melted, mixed and heated to give an explosive force.

> **"a sense of confusion hangs about him"**

The play opens with Reverend Parris 'evidently' in prayer, and this opening action defines the over-riding **religious** **atmosphere** of the drama. Miller's use of the word '**evidently**' in the stage directions is significant, perhaps suggesting that his prayers are not real. Certainly, there are many events and accusations

Explore

Can you find more
evidence in the play
of Parris's lack of
personal beliefs,
which lead to his role
in the witch-hunts?

in the play that are based on things which are <u>not</u> <u>real</u> <u>or</u> <u>not</u> <u>true</u>. The praying of Reverend Parris, together with his weeping and his confusion, helps to reveal his nature. He seems <u>desperate</u> <u>and</u> <u>almost</u> <u>hysterical</u> – a small taste of emotions which are developed later in the play by other characters.

At the beginning there are only two characters on stage, Reverend Parris and his ten-year-old daughter Betty, who is lying in a coma-like state in bed. Tituba's interruption establishes a pattern of <u>hurried</u> <u>entrances</u> <u>and</u> <u>exits</u> in this Act. We later discover that this room is effectively a <u>prison</u> for Parris, who is afraid to go downstairs, because he will be confronted by parishioners accusing him of harbouring witchcraft.

> **❝My Betty not goin' die❞**

Tituba's <u>concern</u> <u>for</u> <u>her</u> <u>ward</u> is plain to see, and we are told that she enters because she 'can no longer bear to be barred from the sight of her beloved'. Perhaps this also presents evidence of a <u>guilty</u> <u>conscience</u> – after all, Betty's 'illness' is a direct result of Tituba's own demonic activities the night before.

Reverend Parris reacts with fury when Tituba expresses hope that his daughter will not die. He cannot cope with such an interruption when he is <u>immersed</u> <u>in</u> <u>his</u> <u>own</u> <u>problems</u>. This is the first of many examples of <u>violence</u>, both verbal and physical, in the play.

Explore

Why do you think
Parris is so afraid:
'quaking with fear'?
What else might he
be scared of?

There also seems to be a contradiction between Parris's prayers for God to help him and the pleas he makes directly to Betty to awake and open her eyes. On one hand we see him as a genuine God-fearing man, on the other as a helpless and desperate father.

The stage note for Abigail gives a <u>contradictory</u> view of her character. Her <u>beauty</u> is important because it helps to explain why John Proctor was tempted by her, but more significant is her 'endless' <u>talent</u> <u>for</u> <u>pretence</u> <u>and</u> <u>deception</u>. This immediately sets her up as someone who <u>readily</u> <u>tells</u> <u>lies</u> and is <u>capable</u> <u>of</u> <u>altering</u> <u>her</u> <u>appearance</u>. The events which unfold reveal this to be more than simply a way of causing harmless mischief. A combination of 'fear' and 'dissembling' has catastrophic results for the community of Salem.

Susanna is the first to mention that the root of Betty's illness might be something supernatural: '<u>You</u> <u>might</u> <u>look</u> <u>to</u> <u>unnatural</u> <u>things</u>'. Parris informs the audience that Reverend Hale has been sent for, a man who will 'look to medicine' to find a cure. His instant, vehement rejection of an 'unnatural' explanation shows how abhorrent it is to him. The fact that it is dismissed immediately suggests that he cannot even bear to contemplate such a thing. It is interesting to trace the steps by which he comes to adopt a different attitude and joins in the persecution of the witches.

Notice how <u>commanding</u> Abigail is when she tells Susanna forcefully, 'speak nothin' of it in the village'. Already we can see that she is <u>in</u> <u>control</u> and apparently the strongest of the local group of girls. It is not difficult to anticipate that she is the <u>ringleader</u> and the dominant character in these events. Abigail is quite <u>brazen</u> in her admittance of the activities the night before, but refutes rumours of witchcraft and suggests that Reverend Parris should confront his congregation. At this stage, Abigail perhaps senses that it would be more in her interest to scotch the rumours of witchcraft.

The stage directions tell us that Parris is '<u>pressed</u>', which suggests that he finds the suggested course of action unattractive.

Explore

Find out what you can about Puritanism. What rules and regulations were people obliged to live by?

His disclosure that he discovered his daughter and Abigail dancing in the forest reveals his fears. In a Puritan society, all <u>acts</u> of <u>entertainment</u> such as <u>dancing were severely frowned upon</u>. Such night-time cavortings would have been viewed with shock and deep suspicion. Pretending to have a fit helps Betty, for the moment, to escape the immediate consequences of her actions and appeases her guilty conscience.

Interestingly, Parris reveals that Betty has been unable to move 'since midnight'. Traditionally, midnight was referred to as 'the witching hour', since it was believed that this was the time when witches and demonic spirits were abroad.

The things that are important to Reverend Parris are made clear: he is <u>afraid</u> of <u>ruin and afraid for himself</u>. This helps to throw light on our first view of him, sobbing and quaking with fear. His words, with their frequent use of personal pronouns such as 'God help me', 'my daughter', 'my niece', 'my enemies', show his <u>self-centredness</u>.

Parris claims that certain factions are sworn to drive him from his pulpit. It is interesting to note that even in an intensely religious society, there are still <u>divisions and factions between people</u>. Clearly, this town is not as wholesome and serene as it initially seems. These latent antagonisms later escalate once the witch-hunt takes hold.

> ❝*Your name in the town – it is entirely white, is it not?*❞

Abigail's account of what happened in the forest may be a reasonable description of the likely sequence of events, but Reverend Parris declares his <u>concerns about whether she will be believed</u>. He urges her to speak the truth: '<u>I pray you feel the weight of truth upon you</u>'. The 'weight of truth' takes on a

Text commentary

more sinister and literal meaning later in the play. How many characters in the play are willing to carry the 'weight of truth'? For now, Parris's statement is ironic – truth is something that Abigail values less than self-preservation. In the same way, Parris wishes not so much for the truth as for his own salvation.

<u>Abigail's</u> <u>reactions</u> <u>quickly</u> <u>change</u> <u>from</u> <u>'innocence'</u> <u>to</u> <u>'terror'</u> once she realises what Parris has actually seen. This could be the turning point for Abigail. Up until now she has been content to brazen out the accusations of dancing and singing, but now her uncle admits to seeing one girl naked, she knows that there can be no harmless explanation. This might go some way to explaining her actions at the end of this Act.

❝❝*There be no blush about my name*❞❞

Reverend Parris's question about Abigail's reputation in the town is the first reference to the importance of '<u>name</u>' in this community. Significantly, Abigail resents the suggestion that her name and identity are being compromised in the eyes of local people. She protests here that there is <u>no stain</u> on her character. Compare these words with Elizabeth Proctor's later reference to Abigail as '<u>something soiled</u>', which suggests the exact opposite. This information also hints at the underlying cause of the tension between Abigail, John Proctor and his wife. The stage directions say that Abigail becomes more and more annoyed, and she uses words such as 'hate', 'bitter' and 'lying' when referring to Elizabeth. Consider the extent to which anger, as well as fear, affects her reactions.

Explore

Elizabeth Proctor is referred to as 'Goody', which is short for 'Goodwife'. What does this reveal about the expected role of wives in this society?

This is a small, <u>close-knit community</u> where everybody knows, or tries to know, his or her neighbour's business. Abigail's dismissal from the Proctors' house clearly generated <u>rumours</u>. The longer she remains unemployed, the sharper such <u>gossip</u> will become, and the more bitterly Abigail will feel it. This may explain why she is so violent in her outburst.

❝It is surely a stroke of hell upon you❞

The entry of the <u>Putnams</u> signals an intensification of the pressures on Parris. Mr Putnam is no friend to him, and Mrs Putnam is a bitter woman, a '<u>twisted</u> <u>soul</u> <u>...</u> <u>haunted</u> <u>by</u> <u>dreams</u>', with a history of bearing children who die immediately after birth. The allegation of witchcraft in the forest has spread. It is ironic that Parris had not seen fit to take Abigail's advice and confront the people with the truth about what happened in the forest. Now he is forced to tell the truth anyway. <u>His</u> <u>desire</u> <u>to</u> <u>protect</u> <u>himself</u> <u>has</u> <u>led</u> <u>to</u> <u>the</u> <u>very</u> <u>opposite</u> <u>of</u> <u>what</u> <u>he</u> <u>wished</u>.

The stage direction 'with vicious certainty' gives information about <u>Mrs</u> <u>Putnam</u>, who seems to welcome the possibility that there might be witchcraft in Salem, and perhaps sees in it an explanation for her misfortunes in being unable to give birth to healthy children. She certainly seems to relish talking about all <u>the</u> <u>horrors</u> <u>of</u> <u>demonic</u> <u>possession</u>, referring to flying, the 'devil's touch', 'death', 'forked and hoofed' and her daughter's soul being 'taken'.

Explore

What are your initial impressions of Mrs Putnam? Can you understand why she acts the way she does? Do we have any sympathy for her?

Mrs Putnam symbolises the worst kind of <u>sensationalist</u> <u>scandal-mongering</u> <u>and</u> <u>hysterical</u> <u>gossip-spreading</u>. In addition, the Putnams have many enemies in Salem: there have been disputes about the selection of the minister, and they have been grasping in land disputes. It is ironic that Mrs Putnam, whose family is later prominent in the witch-hunt, is the first person revealed as having consulted a 'witch' (she sent Ruth to see Tituba in order to consult the dead).

❝They will howl me out of Salem for such corruption in my house❞

Parris is not at all concerned about the truth of the charges of witchcraft, only about the dangers they pose to <u>his</u> <u>own</u>

reputation. Mrs Putnam's emotive language, 'murdered my babies', is echoed in Putnam's accusation that there is a 'murdering witch among us'. Perhaps it is at this stage that the 'conversion' of Parris to the ranks of the witch-hunters begins. His hopes of keeping the scandal away from his own doorstep have been dashed by the Putnams, who seem to have a vested interest in pursuing any witches there might be in Salem.

Abigail is the first to demonstrate the effects of fear, immediately denying her own part in the dancing episode and accusing others, 'Not I, sir – Tituba and Ruth', a pattern which will be followed by many in the ensuing witch-hunt.

The description of Mercy Lewis as 'merciless' in the stage directions reflects ironically on her name. She has come to see Betty, not out of concern for her, but to enjoy the spectacle.

"Have you tried beatin' her?"

When the Putnams depart, Abigail's conversation with Betty and Mercy Lewis reveals further details of what happened in the forest, and tells us more about the girls. Mercy is confident and sly, cruel towards Betty, and perhaps a rather frightening character. She suggests hitting Betty and claims she has already tried that tactic with Ruth. However, there are signs even at this early stage that Abigail has the real power. She holds Mercy back, not out of concern for Betty, but because she is smart enough to be afraid of being found out. She colludes with Mercy so they can get their story straight.

While they are in discussion, Mary Warren arrives. The description of Mary's character is important. Her naivety, loneliness and subservience make it easy for others to influence her, and she falls easy prey to the demands of Abigail and Mercy. Mercy's comment about Mary's 'grand peeping courage' should be kept in mind later, when John Proctor attempts to use her as a witness against the other girls.

'I told him everything'

The interrogation of Betty shows Abigail's <u>ruthlessness</u>. Miller connects her with <u>violent and aggressive actions</u>: 'furiously shakes her', 'beat', 'smashes her across the face'. Betty reveals Abigail's <u>sinister</u> role in the previous evening's events: '<u>you drank blood, Abby!</u> ... <u>You drank a charm to kill Goody Proctor</u>'. This is an important allegation and reminds us of Abigail's earlier hatred of Mrs Proctor.

Abigail has now reached a point where she is forced by events to <u>threaten the other girls into silence</u>, something she does with relative ease. All the girls recognise that they are <u>guilty</u>, and Abigail makes sure she refers to them as 'we' so that they are <u>united in their deeds</u>. She has no qualms about frightening them by mentioning her own brutal past, '<u>I saw Indians smash my dear parents' heads</u>', and hinting that she is capable of such evil deeds herself.

The meeting of the 'witches' is brought to a close by the arrival of John Proctor. Abigail's rude imperative to Mary to 'shut it' is appropriate, bearing in mind that it is Proctor who later persuades Mary to give evidence against the other girls.

The past relationship between Abigail and John Proctor is revealed, but now he rejects her advances. Their relationship is suggested in various ways: Abigail looks at him wide-eyed; she refers to his strength; she laughs nervously; she has a 'winningly ... wicked air'. There is clearly <u>an unspoken bond between them</u>. John is curious about the mischief that Reverend Parris might be brewing. Abigail, however, is implying that he wanted to see her. This scene was not in the original performances, but was added by Miller to give the play more human warmth and emotion – something that it had been criticised for lacking.

We have now seen Abigail in a number of different
emotional conditions. She is <u>volatile</u> and therefore very
dangerous. Her coarse references to Proctor's passionate
approaches – 'I have a sense for heat', 'clutched my back'
and 'sweating like a stallion' – confirms the <u>animal
attraction</u> she finds in John Proctor. She is earthy, very sexual
and does not shy away from tempting John by referring to past
passionate encounters. Her remarks also suggest that <u>John
Proctor</u> <u>is</u> <u>no</u> <u>angel</u>.

> ❝*You'll speak nothin' of Elizabeth!*❞

Abigail cannot resist talking about Goody Proctor as
'sickly', 'cold' and 'snivelling'. John is furious and this
<u>first</u> <u>sign</u> <u>of</u> <u>anger</u> is manifested by his physical
shaking of Abigail, which further underlines the
physical nature of their former relationship. Abigail's
reference to the lying and pretence of the people of
Salem registers the <u>discrepancy</u> <u>between</u> <u>the</u> <u>community's</u>
<u>Christian</u> <u>appearance</u> <u>and</u> <u>its</u> <u>very</u> <u>unchristian</u> <u>reality</u>.

John makes a move to depart, an action that would appear
dramatically ambiguous. It could be because he is disgusted
with Abigail's fevered beliefs, or simply because he knows he has
no answer for her accusations. Either way, events ensure that he
does not leave the stage.

<u>Rebecca</u> <u>Nurse</u> <u>and</u> <u>Giles</u> <u>Corey</u> now appear. Both are
well-respected figures in the community, although
disliked by the Putnams. Abigail is quick to offer the
sound of the congregation's singing as a reason for Betty
crying out. However, Mrs Putnam makes the very damaging
connection between it and witchcraft.

> ❝*they will run the Devil bowlegged
> keeping up with their mischief*❞

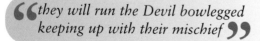

Rebecca is sympathetic to Betty's illness, and her plea for quiet provides a strong contrast to the hectic action which has surrounded the girl's sick-bed so far. Rebecca has Betty's welfare at the front of her mind and brings her temporary relief. This contrasts strongly with the reasons why many of the others are there. She is also perceptive in her understanding of young teenage girls.

Note how Corey cannot keep his mouth shut. As the stage directions indicate, he is very inquisitive, verging on the mischievous, although without any evil intent.

Rebecca's excellent advice, to send Reverend Hale back where he came from, is rejected. Her reference to 'arguin' again in the society' alerts us to the fact that Salem is already split by disputes, and the subsequent discussion between the men confirms this. Rebecca's observation that before looking for outward causes of evil you should examine your own heart and conscience, is met with straight resistance from these self-centred people. We get the impression that they are nervous of looking too closely at their own actions and beliefs.

Mrs Putnam's bitterness, the result of her loss of many children, causes her to round on Rebecca. Look at her ominous references to 'wheels within wheels' and 'fires within fires', both of which are redolent of the fires of hell and the trials of purgatory.

66 *We vote by name in this society* 99

John Proctor reintroduces the theme of 'name', a concept that will grow in importance as the play progresses. 'Name' here signifies the right to an equal voice in the community's affairs, and implies that 'name' only carries weight if its owner is a respected man.

The discussion between Proctor and Parris about sermons highlights the serious rifts in their society. Their laws deal not only with the usual matters like theft, but also with such matters as attendance at church. It indicates, too, that this society is gradually reaching that point when it begins to look beyond the strict conventions which had supported and protected it during the difficult period of settlement in New England.

Text commentary

A change in atmosphere follows the entrance of Reverend Hale, which marks another stage in the **growing momentum** of the action. He immediately stakes his claim to a **position** of **authority**. Note, however, that his 'authority' is **contained** **only** **in** **books** and that h fails to look deeper to find out why these events are occurring. Is he blinded by the 'weight', or authority, of his books? Remember that Dr Griggs could not find an answer to Betty's illness in his books.

He don't believe in witches

Giles Corey cannot resist the temptation to make a mischievous remark about Proctor and witches, but does not cause real harm on this occasion. This is one habit he will come to regret bitterly later in the play. Corey's curiosity prevents him from leaving with John Proctor and brings him misfortune.

Explore

Do you think events might have taken a different turn if Proctor had stayed at this point? What might he have been able to do?

Common sense is something that very few people in Salem seem to possess. John Proctor obviously doesn't believe Betty's illness to be the result of witchcraft. Proctor leaves to continue with his work, getting tired of the never-ending talk of the devil, and also because he holds Reverend Parris and the Putnams in some contempt. Unfortunately, he underestimates the damage they might do.

We cannot look to superstition in this

The Puritans relied on <u>simple</u> <u>interpretations</u> <u>of the Bible</u>. They would have been very familiar with the text '<u>You shall</u> <u>not allow a sorceress to live</u>' (Exodus 22:18), and would find nothing strange in the notion of there being witches to be found. These Puritan characters believe that '<u>the Devil</u> <u>is precise</u>', and when they are convinced that they have discovered signs of witchcraft, it will be almost impossible to turn them from their beliefs or their determined course of action.

> 66 *Here is all the invisible world,*
> *caught, defined, and calculated* 99

Note the obvious <u>respect, almost worship, for the</u> <u>'authority' of the written word</u> as they wait to be enlightened by Reverend Hale. Perhaps we should not judge Reverend Hale too harshly for his obvious delight in being the 'expert' and <u>centre of attention</u>. (Consider Abigail later in the Act.) Most people enjoy being able to demonstrate a particular expertise. What is more worrying is that Hale has an <u>unshakeable belief in his books</u> and cannot see that interpretations may vary. You should bear in mind Hale's sense of authority and superiority when judging the difficult task he has later – when he has to come to terms with the gradual realisation that, despite all his expertise in the subject, he may have made a terrible mistake.

> 66 *we may open up the boil*
> *of all our troubles today* 99

The fact that Parris is '<u>striving for conviction</u>' suggests that he is not so sure about being able to 'catch devils' as the others are, despite his 'hushed' respect for Hale's books. On the other hand, throughout this scene words like 'trepidation', 'fright' and 'fearfully' are applied to him, so he is <u>clearly shaken and uncertain</u>. His comment (above) has an ironic twist. Miller's use of the image of a 'boil'

suggests a festering sore, the visible, outward sign of an inner infection. Rather than cleansing the wound, however, the actions of the townspeople simply inflame it.

Throughout, <u>Rebecca shows a dignity and common sense sadly lacking in the majority of the characters</u>, especially those in 'authority'.

Having seen the respect in which books are held, Giles suddenly introduces a jarring note of contrast: '<u>What signifies the readin' of strange books?</u>'. Traditionally, the Bible was known as '<u>the good book</u>'; Hale's books would certainly be worthy tomes. Giles's description of how he was suddenly able to pray when his wife stopped reading reminds us of Betty's wailing at the sound of the psalms. Unfortunately, Giles is not to realise until too late the foolishness of his continual questions.

66 *Did you call the Devil last night?* 99

The tone becomes more urgent when Parris betrays the crucial evidence that there was a <u>kettle</u> in the grass. This is unmistakably linked to witchcraft, with its <u>cauldron connotations</u>. It also suggests the boiling heat of the <u>crucible</u> itself. In such containers, animals and parts of animals would be mixed with other – often revolting – objects to produce a brew to be used in making magic and casting spells. From here, the <u>momentum is unstoppable</u>. Though Abigail will accept no blame herself, her evidence condemns the girls. Miller judges the pace of this scene masterfully by introducing a series of short, one-sentence utterances and exclamations. The constant question and answer pattern, coupled with the increasing violence of Abigail's replies, speeds up the action and creates a sense of an unstoppable force, which is rapidly racing out of control.

Explore

Originating in Greek drama, the word 'stichomythia' refers to a series of single lines spoken by alternate characters. Can you find other examples of this in the play?

Parris, whose memory of actual events is unclear, seems to give Hale the answer which he thinks he wants, rather than describing what he actually saw. (It is perhaps significant, however, that Parris recalls seeing his niece and 'ten or twelve' other girls 'dancing in the forest'. The number thirteen has obviously sinister and supernatural connotations.) This foreshadows later events, when others give the answers they think are wanted by their questioners, rather than the truth.

Under direct attack from Hale, Abigail looks for a way out. The talk of devils, and the fact that she is once again the centre of an interrogation, makes her desperate. Tituba's reappearance is a welcome relief which turns the spotlight away from Abigail. In selfish desperation, Abby has no hesitation in planting the blame squarely on Tituba's shoulders, even embellishing to the point where Tituba is made to seem like a powerful, tempting sorceress. We can also note that it is typical of Abigail that she cannot help using her own sexuality, telling the reverends that she was made to stand with 'not a stitch on [her] body'.

66 *She beg me to make charm* –99

Explore

Do you think it unfair that Tituba should be blamed? Consider the nature of Salem society and Tituba's position as a slave.

Tituba makes a genuine response to Abigail's accusation. Her interrogation sets a pattern that is repeated later. When people are accused of witchcraft, they begin by denying it, but when they sense that their denials are useless, they usually acknowledge their 'sin', plead for forgiveness and accuse others in the hope of saving themselves. Abigail cunningly takes the initiative here. Her accusation that Tituba makes her laugh when at prayer is quickly confirmed by the Reverend Parris. Cleverly, Abigail uses her own failings to implicate Tituba.

When Hale tells Tituba to let 'God's holy light' shine on her, and asks her whether the devil ever comes 'with another person', it is a key moment. He gives her the opportunity to accuse someone else and she soon senses that if she gives a name, her own case will be helped. The <u>metaphor</u> of <u>darkness</u> significantly introduces the idea of the truth being obscured, as well as the blackness of people's hearts, that they can stand by and watch innocent people being victimised.

Notice that it is Putnam who first suggests the names of Sarah Good and Goody Osburn. This is the first <u>naming of another with malicious intent</u>. At this stage it is difficult to know whether Putnam seeks the death of his victim, but later those making accusations will know what is likely to happen to the people they accuse of being witches. It is perhaps inevitable that Sarah Good is the first name Tituba gives, as Putnam has already suggested it.

❝*I want to open myself!*❞

How do you view this crying out? What might Betty's motivation be?

Perhaps Abigail is afraid that she will be named by Tituba, or perhaps, understanding the mood in the room, she merely grasps her only chance of escape. In another reference to light, the stage directions tell us: '<u>She is enraptured, as though in a pearly light</u>.' Abigail accuses Bridget Bishop to prove that she, too, has information for the interrogators. Betty's sudden interruption has an electrifying effect on the company; Reverend Hale and the others see it as proof that the children were indeed bewitched and that the spell is now broken. The key to Abigail's outburst is seen in the stage direction '<u>great glee</u>'. She enjoys this moment. Suddenly, she is no longer subject to interrogation or under threat of a whipping, but commands everyone's attention and it is they who are under her influence (or her 'spell').

The end of this first Act is particularly chilling, with Abigail emerging as an apparently <u>holy figure</u>, claiming divine inspiration for her accusations of others. The <u>hysteria</u> welling up within the girls is a foretaste of the dramatic end to Act 3, particularly with Miller's use of repetition, each sentence ending with an exclamation and the word 'Devil'. The fall of the curtain on the girls' 'ecstatic cries' is redolent of a <u>tribal frenzy</u>.

A process of elimination

Delete two of the three alternatives given to find the correct plot.

1   *The play is set in 1962/1692/1269.*

2   *Reverend Parris is praying by his daughter's/niece's/servant's bed.*

3   *Abigail/Mercy/Susanna warns the other girls to say nothing.*

4   *John Proctor has slept with Betty/Abigail/Mercy.*

5   *Only Rebecca/Giles/Proctor can calm Betty.*

6   *Abigail accuses Mercy/Betty/Tituba of being a witch.*

Who? What? Why? When? Where? How?

1   *Who sends for Reverend Hale?*

2   *What is John Proctor's job?*

3   *How did Abigail's parents die?*

4   *How do we know the Reverend Hale is a learned man?*

Who is this?

1   *'a subservient, naive, lonely girl'*

2   *'a strikingly beautiful girl, an orphan, with an endless capacity for dissembling'*

3   *'a fat, sly, merciless girl of eighteen'*

4   *'a secret child ... [she] shrivels like a suckling mouth were pullin' on her life too'*

5   *'She were swaying like a dumb beast over that fire!'*

Take a moment to consider ...

Why do you think Miller calls Act 1 'An Overture'?

Text commentary

Act 2

It is evening, eight days after the events of Act 1. Continuing the **enclosed atmosphere** of the previous scene, Act 2 is set in the main room of John Proctor's house. At first, the action is centred on John and his wife Elizabeth. **Affairs which touch them are symptomatic of the wider events which affect the whole of Salem**.

> **❝ *It's well seasoned* ❞**

The opening scene says something about the relationship between John and Elizabeth Proctor. Abigail earlier described Elizabeth as a 'cold' woman, and John Proctor defended his wife. Now we have an opportunity to judge Elizabeth for ourselves. John's action in seasoning the food to his taste without his wife's knowledge, then complimenting her on how well she has judged the seasoning, shows **his wish that she should be happy**. It also shows a **lack of honesty** in the relationship. Her reaction indicates a corresponding **desire to please him**.

The stew is made from a rabbit which has walked into the house, which is 'a good sign' according to John. This directly contrasts with the frog which Abigail claimed had jumped into the kettle and which Hale suspected could be a sign of dealing with the Devil. Throughout this Act, you are reminded of the difference between Abigail and Elizabeth.

The stilted conversation and the stage directions provide **jarring notes** in the peacefully domestic scene. Elizabeth 'receives' his kiss. There is **no sense of any warmth** between the couple, despite her pleasure at his compliment about the meal. John's relationship with Abigail obviously still comes between him and Elizabeth. They warily walk around each other, unable to say out loud what they really think and feel. This lack of honesty between the two illustrates, in microcosm, the ill that affects the whole community.

66 Lilac is the smell of nightfall 99

We see John's sensuous side in his language. He is a farmer, in tune with the countryside and changing seasons. His comment about the lack of flowers in his house, 'It's winter in here yet', also symbolises the coldness Elizabeth brings to the marriage.

66 It is a mouse no more 99

Explore

Research the Biblical story surrounding this Red Sea image. What does it suggest about the way people are viewing Abigail?

Mary Warren's change from timidity to arrogance reflects a change in the atmosphere in Salem. Elizabeth's sarcastic remarks about Abigail being a 'saint', and of the crowds parting for her 'like the sea for Israel' indicate the power that she has gained in only eight days.

Explore

What are the various reasons why John is unwilling to take action?

John ignores Elizabeth's suggestion that he should go to Ezekiel Cheever to expose the girls' lies in court. Instead, later in this Act, Ezekiel comes for Elizabeth. This is the first real test for John. If he had gone to Cheever some days earlier, events might have turned out differently.

66 it is not as you told me 99

The realisation that John was alone in the room with Abigail, and that he has therefore lied to her, comes as a shock to Elizabeth and shakes her confidence in him. John is in a hopeless situation – no matter what he does he will lose. He has deceived his wife about his latest meeting with Abigail, afraid that it would further damage his relationship with her, and if he proceeds with the course of action Elizabeth suggests, going voluntarily before the court, much more may be disclosed. If he doesn't, it will confirm what she obviously already suspects.

> **The magistrate sits in your heart that judges you**

The accuracy of Elizabeth's remark is shown later when John has to face up to the consequences of his actions and act according to his own conscience. Her comment that he is a 'good man' shows her underlying faith in him despite his unfaithfulness. Her belief in his innate honesty is again shown in Act 4, when she refuses to advise him on what he ought to do.

Mary Warren's arrival interrupts the mutual recriminations between John and Elizabeth, and delays Proctor's decision about going to Cheever with his account of Abigail's confessions.

> **I'll whip you if you dare leave this house again!**

Explore

This is a violent society. What other examples of whipping are mentioned in the text?

The implication in this comment is that John has been violent to Mary in the past. It is plain that his argument with Elizabeth has angered him, perhaps because he has no real answer to her criticisms. With Mary's return, he has the opportunity to vent some of his anger.

Mary's repeated cry, 'I am sick, I am sick', could be assumed out of fear or might be the result of auto-suggestion. Is the sickness physical or spiritual? Mary is no longer the arrogant girl who, earlier that day, informed Elizabeth that she must be about the court's work. It is clear that the events which she has witnessed have had a profound effect on her. Her remark that they must 'all love each other now' is strange, perhaps suggesting

Explore

Research the use of dolls in witchcraft.

that John Proctor should be more careful in his attitude towards her. Her present of the doll becomes the most significant factor in Elizabeth's arrest.

"Goody Osburn – will hang!"

Explore

Watch the film of *The Crucible* (1996) for which Arthur Miller wrote the screenplay. It contains extra scenes in court, which effectively show the hysteria and hypocrisy.

The news that 39 people have been arrested shows that the witch-hunt is growing in momentum. The news that Goody Osburn is sentenced to death is 'balanced' by the fact that Sarah Good has confessed and will not hang. Mary feels Sarah's confession helps to 'justify' the death sentence passed on Goody Osburn. Later, when Danforth strives for John Proctor's confession, he sees it as a partial 'justification' for the trials and hangings that have already taken place in Salem.

Explore

What other examples can you find in the play of unlikely or unconvincing things being believed?

The description of how Mary came to condemn Goody Osburn shows the extent of the girls' hysteria. Their dancing in the forest has put them in a situation from which they cannot escape. Throughout this scene, the most ominous, even terrifying, aspect is the credulity which the court shows in hearing evidence. It seems that simply by confessing, a 'witch' can escape hanging, which strongly induces these simple folk to confess to crimes they did not commit.

"It's strange work for a Christian girl to hang old women!"

Mary's proud exclamation that she is 'an official of the court' is now joined by her claim to be doing 'God's work'. This is an example of the hypocrisy of Salem society. Her claim does not impress John, and his determination to whip her is prevented only by her disclosure that Elizabeth is under threat.

"I saved her life today!"

Mary does not directly say that Elizabeth was accused of being a witch, but uses the euphemistic phrase that she was 'somewhat mentioned'. This is repeated in relation to Rebecca Nurse in Act 3.

Text commentary

Mary does not say that Abigail made the accusation against Elizabeth, but both Elizabeth and John assume that it was her. This new threat subdues and shocks both of them.

Note how the action has led up to this moment. Elizabeth and John have been trying to come to terms with his infidelity, but fail to reach agreement. Mary's news makes them forget their own concerns for a while, but when they learn that Elizabeth has been accused, John's relationship with Abigail is brought back to mind.

Elizabeth realises the danger of her situation and how much she needs John's testimony against Abigail. His position in society is such that an accusation made against his wife has more significance than those made against Goody Osburn and Sarah Good. Now that his wife is under threat from the witch-hunt, <u>John has to make a decision</u>: either he openly admits his guilt and sacrifices his good name, or he allows his wife to be accused as a witch.

❝ _I'll not be ordered to bed no more_ ❞

Mary's petulance reminds us that the key figures in the trial are <u>just children</u>, which makes their accusations of witchcraft against others all the more horrifying and unnatural. Elizabeth realises that one of these children, Abigail, plans to take her place in the marriage.

Explore

Does John still have feelings for Abby? Has she still got 'an arrow' in him as Elizabeth suspects?

The repetition of the stallion image, 'The promise that a stallion gives a mare I gave that girl', reminds us of when it was first used by Abigail to John in Act 1, to show his strong desire for her. Note that <u>animal imagery</u> is often used in the play, which is appropriate for a farming community.

When Hale arrives, he appears 'drawn', with <u>a quality of</u> <u>'deference, even of guilt'</u>, suggesting a major change from the Reverend Hale we met in Reverend Parris's house. This guilt may suggest his dawning realisation that all these people cannot really be tainted with witchcraft.

John's nervousness, 'We're not used to visitors after dark', helps to remind us of the setting of the play and the way <u>the community feels threatened by the wilderness surrounding it</u>. Ironically, the greatest threat to the community comes from within.

> 66 *I come of my own, without the court's authority* 99

Reverend Hale's revelation that his visit is without the court's authorisation indicates that <u>his faith in the justice of the court's proceedings has been severely shaken</u>. Hale, a stranger to this community, wishes to carry out a personal investigation at the Proctors' house away from the hysteria that surrounds the court proceedings, thereby demonstrating his <u>personal integrity</u>.

In so divided a society it is perhaps unsurprising that over 30 people have so far have been accused. <u>The court presents an opportunity for outstanding feuds and debts to be settled</u> and personal hatred to be vented. The situation is getting out of hand, as illustrated by the news that the good Rebecca Nurse is now being implicated in witchcraft. In this society, there is no distinction between a person's duty to the state and to God.

Explore

Does John really forget his Commandments, or can he not bring himself to say the words because he has sinned against them?

The deep rift between John and Parris is highlighted by the disclosure that John's third child has not been baptised, because he feels that <u>there is no 'light of God' in Parris</u>, a serious charge against a minister. In the Ten Commandments test John forgets '<u>Thou shall not</u>

commit adultery', which is ironic in the light of his recent discussion with his wife. Hale's suspicion of the Proctors is intensified by John's forgetfulness. Witch-hunts are conducted on petty pretexts such as this.

> **I think you must tell him, John**

It is Elizabeth who brings up the subject of Abigail, just as Hale is about to depart. John seems to be backing away from the ordeal of exposing his human frailties and sins before his fellow citizens. When asked why he had not revealed his knowledge about the adventure in the woods before, John is unable to answer honestly. There is some truth in his reply that he had not realised until then how far events had progressed, but his answer contains an element of deception, not only of Reverend Hale, but possibly of himself.

> **There are them that will swear to anything before they'll hang**

John hits on a crucial weakness of a judicial system which exploits the fear of the accused: where a confession enables the accused to escape hanging, a lie may guarantee safety. His defence of Elizabeth, 'A woman that never lied, and cannot', paves the way for the climax in Act 3 when John's fate hangs on Elizabeth always telling the truth.

Giles Corey's and Francis Nurse's arrival with the news of fresh arrests increases the sense of expectancy about the Proctors' fate. Now a climate has been created in which no-one is safe from accusation and arrest. Hale is troubled by the news, but continues to believe the evidence brought to court. Note the absurd contrast between the charges, one of murdering babies, the other of the death of a pig. Giles seems to have forgotten that he has brought this trouble on his wife by mentioning to Hale his concern about her reading of books.

The arrival of Marshal Herrick and Cheever brings the events of the previous week to their inevitable conclusion. We should not be surprised that Abigail has brought charges against Elizabeth. Consider how this could have been avoided. Could John Proctor have influenced events? How willing has he been to face up to reality and responsibility?

❝I spy a poppet, Goody Proctor❞

Explore

Why would the authorities rather believe that Elizabeth is possessed by the Devil and guilty of plotting to murder Abigail than that the reverse is true?

The discovery of **the doll** with the needle in it condemns Elizabeth because of the belief in sympathetic magic. The account of Abigail's injury with the needle leaves little doubt as to the purpose of her careful plan. Despite Mary Warren's confession that it is her doll and her needle, and that it was she who brought into the house, Cheever and Hale choose to ignore her. This shows the strength of their fanaticism about hunting down and prosecuting witches.

Proctor's action in **ripping up the warrant** is held against him when he confronts Danforth later. However, the provocation for his action will not be taken into account by the court. This is the mark of a witch-hunt that it is concerned only with appearance rather than with the circumstances or motives which prompted the actions or accusations. By tearing up the Deputy Governor's warrant, John **signals his rejection of the foolishness, fanaticism and hysteria gripping Salem**.

❝the little crazy children are jangling the keys of the kingdom❞

Here John Proctor points out the fundamental weakness in the court's procedure – complete **faith in the accuser's innocence**. He identifies a 'vengeance' ruling Salem, but he fails to mention his own part in allowing it to take root by remaining silent until now.

John draws a parallel between Hale and Pontius Pilate. Research this parallel. Is Hale like Pontius Pilate? Both men commanded positions of power, but has Hale really the power to prevent anything? Has Proctor? Can any individual withstand the tide of hysteria in Salem?

66 *John – I think I must go with them* 99

Elizabeth is a __realist__. She recognises that there is nothing that Proctor can do to prevent her arrest and so she concentrates on making last-minute arrangements for her family. She demonstrates great __self-control__, putting her own safety last.

The absolute certainty which Hale showed at the end of Act 1 no longer seems to be there. He is in a '__fever of guilt and uncertainty__' and John accuses him of being a coward. The earlier arrests of less significant people such as Goody Osburn and Sarah Good may not have moved him much, but the current defendants – Martha Corey, Rebecca Nurse and now Elizabeth Proctor – perhaps give him pause for thought.

66 *Abby'll charge lechery on you* 99

The fact that Mary knows of his relationship with Abigail brings Proctor to an abrupt halt. If Mary knows, who else knows? John Proctor's __guilty secret__ seems to be common knowledge, but __he still has to gain the courage to admit his sin in public__.
He now uses strong religious imagery: 'Hell and Heaven grapple on our backs'; 'God's icy wind'. It is __Proctor's moral duty as a Christian to stop the witch-hunt__. In this final speech of Act 2 he has lost all pretensions and is 'but naked now'. No longer will he have to live a lie with Elizabeth, tormented by his past. He recognises, however, that what is coming will be a great ordeal.

A process of elimination

Delete two of the three alternatives given to find the correct plot.

1   Act 2 is set in the Proctors'/Putnams'/Parris's house.

2   It is two/eight/fourteen days after the last Act.

3   Fourteen/two/twenty people are already in jail.

4   Danforth/Parris/Hale arrives at the house.

5   John forgets the Commandment concerning murder/adultery/theft.

6   John is determined to force Mary to give evidence against Elizabeth/Rebecca/Abigail.

Who? What? Why? When? Where? How?

1   Who does John call 'Pontius Pilate'?

2   Who is clerk of the Salem court?

3   What does Mary give Elizabeth?

4   Why has Rebecca been arrested?

5   How does Mary escape being whipped by John?

6   How does Abigail bring about Elizabeth's arrest?

Who says ... ?

1   'The magistrate sits in your heart that judges you. I never thought you but a good man.'

2   'Theology, sir, is fortress; no crack in a fortress may be accounted small.'

3   'You have a faulty understanding of young girls. There is a promise made in any bed ... spoke or silent, a promise that is surely made.'

Take a moment to consider ...

In what ways is the setting of Act 2 different from that of the other three Acts?

Text commentary

Act 3

Explore

What other staging devices does Miller utilise in the play?

The setting is the vestry room of the Salem meeting house, one week after the events of Act 2. Interestingly, Miller chooses to have this scene begin with '<u>sunlight pouring through two high windows in the back wall</u>'. Perhaps the sunlight suggests to the audience that this is a room where light can be shed on the previous events, or perhaps even that the light of Heaven falls onto the proceedings. In fact, the light brings nothing of the sort and as an audience, like Proctor and Giles, we are <u>lulled into a false sense of security</u>.

> **❝*I have evidence for the court!*❞**

The evidence that <u>Giles Corey</u> wishes to bring before the court is his accusation that '<u>Thomas Putnam is reaching out for land</u>'. In what is supposed to be a harmonious society, it is obvious that there are serious rifts between some of the land-owners. You should look at how the court views Giles's evidence. Do you think the court is only really interested in hearing information from the girls?

Annoyed that his examination of Martha Corey has been interrupted, <u>Hathorne</u> calls for Giles's arrest. Martha Corey's examination illustrates <u>the hopelessness of arguing against convoluted logic</u> – if you do not know what a witch is like, how do you know you are not a witch? Hathorne's attitude to Giles suggests that no sympathetic hearing can ever be expected from him. He is determined that any information must be delivered by the appropriate channels. The stage directions describe Hathorne as '<u>a bitter, remorseless judge</u>', and this opening scene is filled with legal terms and language: 'evidence', 'contentious', 'Supreme court', 'submit' and 'affidavit'.

> **❝❝**exact loyalty to his
> position and his cause**❞❞**

Danforth's 'humour and sophistication' will not interfere with what he considers to be his duty. He believes in what he is doing and can see no wrong in the court's decisions. He seems to have a <u>limited</u> <u>perception</u> <u>of</u> <u>human</u> <u>nature</u> and finds it difficult to conceive that the girls are anything other than what they say they are. He is single-mindedly determined to root out witchcraft and does not want to know about anything which may lead him in a different direction. However, as with Reverend Hale, it is possible that he might be persuaded to listen to other points of view.

The reappearance of Reverend Parris suggests that his fears about the discovery of witchcraft in his own house have not been realised. Far from being hounded from the village, he seems to be at the centre of things, holding sway as an official of the court. Parris's comment about Corey, calling him 'contentious' (liable to argue and speak out of turn), suggests that <u>he</u> <u>allows</u> <u>personal</u> <u>feelings</u> <u>to</u> <u>influence</u> <u>his</u> <u>views</u>, but then, he has a lot to lose.

Giles's reference to books mystifies the judge. Giles perhaps feels that his unguarded remarks to Reverend Hale in Act 1, concerning the effect of his wife reading books, are now the reason for her arrest. Giles's seemingly harmless curiosity appears to have had serious repercussions and he is now clearly regretting his actions.

Reverend Hale's plea that Giles should be heard indicates that the doubts he showed at the end of Act 2 are still present. He is ready to consider evidence which might contradict that of the 'witches'.

"They are all deceiving you"

Francis Nurse attempts to plead his wife's cause. Considering Danforth's chilling response to Giles and rebuff of Reverend Hale, it seems unlikely that this plea will be any more successful than the last. Note that it is only when he condemns the girls as frauds that Danforth takes any notice.

Hathorne refuses to recognise the anguished sincerity of these men and sees them only as a threat to the legal proceedings. Hathorne accuses Giles of being in contempt of court – a direct reaction to the potential threat. When Danforth discloses how many are in jail (nearly 400) and the large number condemned to hang (72) we are reminded of the extent to which the witch-hunt has affected this small Massachusetts community. This is also a dramatic device to indicate that time has passed and that the action has moved on with seemingly unstoppable momentum.

"We burn a hot fire here; it melts down all concealment"

Explore

What 'fire' is Danforth referring to here? Is there any irony in this metaphor?

Giles re-enters at this point, with Proctor and Mary Warren. Mary's statement means that the basis of Danforth's case against the accused – the seeing of spirits – is being challenged by a key witness. No wonder Danforth is surprised and alarmed: this new development is totally unexpected, and the 'seeing' of spirits is a key piece of evidence against most of the accused.

The fierce opposition shown by Reverend Parris to the new turn of events indicates his panic. If the court is overthrown then he will be left on his own again. His charge that Proctor and Mary Warren have 'come to overthrow the court' means that he thinks they are acting against God, since Salem is a theocratic society. If Heaven speaks through the children, anyone who contradicts them is denying Heaven and is uttering <u>blasphemy</u> – a crime as heinous as being a witch, or carrying out a murder, or committing adultery.

Unlike Parris, Danforth appreciates the wider implications of what is happening. His question to John Proctor, 'Have you given out this story in the village?', is the first test of Proctor's intentions. If Proctor had wanted to create a public outcry against the court with a view to overthrowing it by force, he would have attempted to get public opinion onto his side by making public what he knew about Mary. Though Proctor has not adopted this course of action, he is nonetheless sincere about stopping the court, as his insistence on Mary's presence shows.

> **Are you certain in your conscience, Mister?**

Danforth's question to John Proctor is the first open reference to <u>conscience</u>. Proctor may have a clear conscience about the truth of the evidence he brings before the court, but in other respects, particularly regarding his relationship with Abigail, we know that <u>his conscience is not entirely clear</u>.

Unluckily for Proctor, his hasty action in tearing up the warrant helps to destroy his case. From being the accuser, John finds himself being interrogated about his own character. There are parallels here with previous allegations against John, voiced by Reverend Hale. Both Parris and Cheever add to John's discomfort by accusing him of offences against their Sunday observance laws.

> **My wife pregnant!**

The news that Elizabeth is pregnant surprises John and Danforth gives him a difficult choice. If he has come only to save his wife's life, rather than to cause problems for the court proceedings, then the offer to let her live until after the baby is born is attractive, especially as 'a year is long' and many things may happen in the meantime. However, to strike this bargain, Proctor must drop his charges that the girls are lying. If he does this, what of Mary Warren's statement and Corey's and Nurse's wives' testimonies? They will be abandoned to their fate. Proctor faces the first test of his personal integrity and he knows that he <u>must</u> <u>stand</u> <u>by</u> <u>what</u> <u>he</u> <u>personally</u> <u>believes</u> <u>in</u>.

Parris is quick to express his opinion of John. He senses the truth behind Proctor's allegations, and his <u>fear</u> <u>for</u> <u>himself</u> and his position dominates his words and actions. Since the entrance of Proctor and Mary he has been described in stage directions as '<u>in</u> <u>shock</u>' and as '<u>sweating</u>'. There is much evidence in this scene revealing his relationship with Danforth. Does the Deputy Governor respect him? Perhaps more importantly, does Danforth believe him?

Explore

What sort of man do you think Danforth is? What evidence can you find to support your opinion?

Danforth is described as <u>resenting</u> <u>the</u> <u>implication</u> <u>that</u> <u>he</u> <u>cannot</u> <u>recognise</u> <u>a</u> <u>good</u> <u>and</u> <u>worthy</u> <u>man</u>. Compare his response to the interruptions from Giles, Francis and John Proctor with those of Hathorne and Parris.

❝*the devil lives on*❞

The obvious disagreement between Reverend Parris and Reverend Hale strongly contrasts with their first meeting. To a certain extent their roles have been reversed, with Hale almost the sceptic and Parris expressing certainty about the witches in his words, though his manner is often less confident. We are beginning to look at Hale in a different light, admiring both <u>his</u> <u>ability</u> <u>to</u> <u>see</u> <u>where</u> <u>he</u> <u>may</u> <u>have</u> <u>been</u> <u>wrong</u> <u>and</u> <u>his</u> <u>attempts</u> <u>to</u> <u>reverse</u> <u>the</u> <u>situation</u>.

"These people should be summoned"

John produces a list of names from people in the community who have signed a 'testament' declaring their good opinion of the accused. This is a real sign of what a close-knit society ought to be about – **people who are prepared to support each other**. In a clear example of the way **old values are being destroyed**, instead of being praised, Parris wants all 91 signatories arrested and questioned for making an attack on the court. Note the friends' horrified reaction to the disaster their good intentions have brought upon innocent people – clearly they had not anticipated this outcome. Ironically, the deposition will also land Giles, Francis and John Proctor in prison. Giles insists that John hands over his deposition. The effect of this is to leave the audience in suspense while it is read and so heightens the tension.

Significantly, Danforth tells Francis '**this is a sharp time**'. He means that affairs are to be conducted with precision and control, but the inference of this metaphor is far more sinister, having connotations of **blades and ruthless cutting down of innocent people**. It is also reminiscent of Abigail's threat to the girls of 'pointy reckoning'.

The talkativeness of **Giles Corey**, coupled with the fact that he has been to court no less than 33 times and always as the plaintiff, never the accused, tells you a great deal about the man. His deposition is well phrased and he understands the difference between a hearing and a full court session. His obstinacy means that Danforth has to declare the court in full session. Giles's **court experience** is mainly of property disputes, so he is out of his depth here. He is no match for men like Danforth and Putnam, but he has a conscience – unfortunately for him.

When asked for proof of his charge against Putnam, Giles realises that without implicating his informant, his evidence is of no use. As in John's case, <u>his conscience prevents him from abandoning his friend</u> to the mercy of the court in order to save himself and his wife.

You will notice that Giles's manner changes on the entrance of Putnam: his 'ease goes'. Soon he shouts a vulgar insult at him ('a fart on Thomas Putnam'); shortly afterwards he attempts to attack him. <u>Putnam is certainly unpopular</u>, and Giles's view is shared by other characters, if in less extreme form. Although the character of Putnam is only sketched in, resentment of his actions lies behind a considerable part of the factional wrangling in Salem. Danforth calls Giles '<u>a foolish old man</u>'. Is this all there is to be said about the old man, or is there more to him?

Explore

Why do you think Giles has such hatred for Thomas Putnam?

<u>Reverend Hale's peace of mind is disturbed</u> by the actions of the court and by Danforth's declaration that there is a 'moving plot to topple Christ in the country'. Hale, like Danforth, has been <u>impressed by Proctor's evidence and by his calm and dignified manner</u>. This is a different John Proctor from the one we saw in earlier scenes when he was full of anger and self-pity. Hale's sensitivity to what is happening also makes us a little more sympathetic to him, but does this vanish when he reveals that he has just signed Rebecca Nurse's death warrant?

❝❝Let you consider now❞❞

Explore

How does Miller present Mary's character in the play? Look at all the references to her and the scenes in which she appears.

Study the logic of Danforth's argument. Is there any way in which the accusations of the girls can be disproved? <u>The only possibility rests with Mary Warren</u>. Remember how she was first described as a 'subservient, naive, lonely girl'. It is perhaps unrealistic to believe that she might become the instrument of justice and truth, considering her easily influenced, weak nature.

Mary's evidence is damning. Danforth's explanation that whatever she says now, she will still be convicted of lying to the court shows what <u>an impossible situation</u> Mary is in. She sobs, and is clearly frightened. This is a trait we associate with Mary throughout the play – remember how she sobbed as John Proctor threw her to the floor at the end of Act 2.

The argument about the poppet adds a touch of the ridiculous to the proceedings, and John Proctor's comment about the dragon with five legs in his house might have been seen as humorous in a court less fanatical in its zeal to discover witches.

❝I believe she means to murder❞

Reverend Parris reacts swiftly as he sees his own position in the court becoming undermined by John Proctor's words. Just as the attack on Abigail and Parris looks as though it is about to succeed, Hathorne is allowed to turn the inquisition back to Mary Warren. Logically, the admission that he and Parris wrest from her, that <u>she 'cannot faint now'</u>, may seem to be convincing in proving that she is lying when she says it was pretence. Think carefully about Mary's actions. Why do you think she was able to pretend to faint before, but cannot now?

Danforth is struck by Mary's evidence and this is one of the moments when his confidence is shaken, when <u>doubt could lead him to the truth</u>. Abigail's reaction at this stage (she is already known to be guilty of dancing) is therefore critical to the progress of the trial.

❝Let me go, Mr Proctor, I cannot, I cannot❞

When the questioning is turned on Abigail, she knows she has to react quickly and positively to avert danger. For her, <u>the best form of defence is attack</u>. Note the similarities between the way she turns on Danforth and her attack on Tituba near the end of Act 1. <u>Abigail's instinct for self-preservation is very strong</u>.

The effect that Abigail has on Mary is plain. The <u>hysteria</u> which Abigail instantly conjures up is quickly taken up by Mercy Lewis and, faced with these two, Mary has little chance of survival. The power these girls have over others is immense. <u>Danforth is not stupid, yet he is 'engaged and entered by Abigail'</u>. His questions to Mary are the final straw for her. Unable to cope with the constant attack, she attempts to flee and is on the brink of collapse.

66*It is a whore!*99

So far in this Act, there has been no contact between Abigail and John Proctor, but now, sensing that she is about to 'win back' Mary and destroy his case, <u>an overpowering rage grips him</u> and he leaps at Abigail. In the stage directions we learn that he is 'breathless and in agony', 'trembling' and 'feeling that his life [is] collapsing about him'. It is clear that revealing his past indiscretions with Abigail is <u>a terrible confession</u> for him to make, but <u>his conscience will not allow him to keep silent</u> while Abigail looks to be controlling the court.

This is a crucial moment for John Proctor. He knows that acknowledging in public that he is a lecher and an adulterer will shock and outrage the court. His comment to Danforth that <u>a man will not willingly 'cast away his good name'</u> has the ring of truth about it, so that Danforth simply accepts Proctor's declaration as fact. Dramatically, this scene is very important. In this society, a man's 'good name' is crucial: if lost, everything is lost, because 'name' is bound up with social and moral standing.

Abigail attempts to bluster and threaten her way out of the room but fails. Danforth, shaken now by John Proctor's admission of adultery, accepts that there might be substance in his accusation against Abigail. <u>If she is a harlot, the voice of Heaven could not speak through her</u>. He has no option but to test Proctor's allegations.

My husband – is a goodly man, sir

What John Proctor does not foresee is that, for once, Elizabeth will not tell the truth about his relationship with Abigail. <u>Her love for John and desire to make sure his name remains 'clean' forces her to renounce her high morals and lie for his sake</u>. For the past seven months, since he 'confessed' his adultery, Elizabeth and John have lived under great strain. Given the love that Elizabeth has shown for her husband, and the great importance which they give the matter of 'name', is it surprising that she refuses to blacken his name before the court? Once again, John Proctor will be ineffective in putting a stop to the witch-hunt.

Explore

Do Elizabeth's actions make you change your opinion of her?

Trial scenes on stage are usually dramatically effective in their mixture of formality and tension, characters and truths slowly revealed, with the additional suspense as to whether judge and/or jury will respond in the same way as the audience.

For what cause did you dismiss her?

This is <u>an impossible question for Elizabeth</u>. If she tells the truth she condemns her husband as an adulterer, if she lies she goes against the dictates of her own conscience. Her familiarity with the Ten Commandments and her husband's statement that she cannot lie, suggest that she would find the latter very difficult. She also does not know what her husband has said. Does she think that he would not have told the truth, and therefore out of loyalty to him she, too, is driven to tell a lie?

The terrible irony of this question is that a truthful answer from one of the most respected citizens in the community might have brought the whole business to an end. As it is, Elizabeth feels driven to shield her husband and unwittingly destroys his case, thus ensuring that he is arrested and that the witch-hunts continue with increased vigour. <u>This small test of Elizabeth is symbolic of the way that people's lives are now hanging on the right words being spoken</u>. John Proctor's life depended on one word from his wife, but the morals of Salem have become so warped that by lying to protect him she simply condemns him to death.

❝❝*it is a natural lie to tell***❞❞**

Text commentary

You should recognise the importance for Reverend Hale's perception that Elizabeth's was 'a natural lie'. At last it seems Reverend Hale has found his own conscience. Remember that Puritan society lived by rigid adherence to God's law, and <u>to call a lie 'natural' is to flout God's law</u>. Seen in this context, Reverend Hale's comment is extraordinary and shows his development since Act 1.

Reverend Hale's insistence that he can no longer 'shut [his] conscience' indicates his anguish at the way the witch-hunts are being carried out. He is now prepared to defend John and Elizabeth, for he believes that <u>'private vengeance' lies beneath the court charges</u>? This is a dangerous moment for Abigail and the other girls. Hale is a well-respected and important figure in the community, and his opinions carry weight.

Danforth, on the other hand, <u>grasps eagerly at certainty</u>. He has been shaken in his confidence, but now John is seen as a liar according to the rules he has laid down. During the rest of this scene, Danforth, for all his show of authority, his shrewdness in organising the questioning of Elizabeth and his firmness in repulsing Abigail's bluster, is <u>unable to cope with the fear of the unknown</u>.

Abigail's speed in reacting to the threat of Hale again shows her <u>strong</u> <u>sense</u> <u>of</u> <u>self-preservation</u>. Within seconds she reclaims the attention of the court officials. John Proctor desperately tries to counteract her 'spell' when Abigail suggests that Mary Warren is under the influence of evil and that <u>she herself</u> <u>is</u> <u>doing</u> <u>God's</u> <u>work</u> in 'calling out' witches.

Explore

How would you choose to present this scene if you were the director?

The following scene is dramatically very exciting. How does Abigail win the battle for control over Mary? Note that Mary faces pressure from all sides: John Proctor cries that Mary should remember the angel Raphael; Danforth questions her 'an inch from her face'; Reverend Parris urges her to cast the devil out.

If we are to be convinced by the unlikely (though true) events of *The Crucible*, <u>the</u> <u>audience</u> <u>must</u> <u>be</u> <u>convinced</u> <u>equally</u> <u>of</u> <u>the</u> <u>power</u> <u>of</u> <u>hysteria</u>. There are indications of this in various places in the play, but here we find by far the strongest example. We do not know if the girls are pretending. Certainly Abigail knows what she is doing when she first 'sees' the bird but, in a compelling <u>whirl</u> <u>of</u> <u>hysteria</u> <u>and</u> <u>auto-suggestion</u>, soon no-one knows what is or is not. In particular, Proctor's control evaporates into wild blasphemy ('God is dead!') as he contributes to the final collapse of his case.

> ❝*A fire, a fire is burning!*❞

At the end of the Act Miller again uses <u>fire</u> <u>imagery</u>. Contrasting directly with Danforth's 'hot fire' that 'melts down all concealment', Proctor denounces the fires of Salem as Lucifer's (i.e. the Devil's). Far from removing concealment, they help to conceal the falseness in their hearts. This is a powerful condemnation of the court proceedings and those who control them, but, ironically, it reflects the fraud which was in John's own heart.

Text commentary

Quick quiz 3

A process of elimination

Delete two of the three alternatives given to find the correct plot.

1   Proctor brings Elizabeth/Mary/Abigail to the court to testify against the girls.

2   Hale/Hathorne/Danforth offers to let the pregnant Elizabeth live for a year.

3   John gives the judges a testament with 9/ 91/ 191 signatures.

4   Danforth orders all these people to be imprisoned/hanged/arrested for questioning.

5   Elizabeth denies that John is a lecher in order to save his good name/Abigail/herself.

6   Mary/Abigail/Elizabeth, attacked on all fronts, accuses John Proctor.

7   John and Parris/Giles/Hale are arrested.

8   Parris/Giles/Hale denounces the proceedings.

Who? What? Why? When? Where? How?

1   Who threatens Danforth?

2   Who is 'a lump of vanity'?

3   What does Abigail 'see' up in the rafters?

4   Where did John sleep with Abigail?

5   Where does this Act of the play take place?

Who says ... ?

1   'We burn a hot fire here; it melts down all concealment.'

2   'God is dead!'

3   'Do that which is good, and no harm shall come to thee.'

4   'Abby, Abby, I'll never hurt you more!'

Take a moment to consider ...

Images of heat and cold feature in this Act and elsewhere. How far is John associated with heat throughout the play?

Text commentary

Act 4

It is daybreak, some three months later. The scene is a prison cell. Audience anticipation is created because John Proctor does not appear until halfway through the Act. Note the **oppressiveness** of the cell. In contrast to the previous Acts, no sun 'pours' or 'streams' through the windows; no open door gives a glimpse of green fields. The place is in **darkness** and the moonlight merely 'seeps' through the bars.

> ❝*Devil, him be pleasureman in Barbados*❞

Explore

Who is compared to 'some great bird' in this Act? What is the effect of this simile?

Sarah and Tituba talk of a '**devil bird**', a reminder of the 'bird' that Abigail and the others saw at the end of Act 3. Is the 'devil' that they talk about the same devil which the court would recognise? Tituba's devil seems to have an **air of joy**: perhaps she is right when she says that such a devil would find its 'soul' frozen in Massachusetts.

Tituba mistaking a bellowing cow for Satan ('I'm here, Majesty!') adds **light relief** before the tension and tragedy of what is to follow. It also makes the serious point that during this witch-hunt it was all too easy to misinterpret innocent events as devilish ones.

> ❝*He goes among them that will hang*❞

Reverend Hale is still out of favour with the authorities, yet he has returned to Salem and sits and prays with the condemned, showing that he retains **a sense of responsibility** for the demands of his ministry. We learn that he pleads with Rebecca and others that they will confess their crimes and so escape hanging. Whereas previously he was concerned solely with <u>saving souls</u> and driving out the Devil, now he aims to <u>save lives</u>.

Hathorne's reference to Parris's 'mad' look suggests that Parris, too, has been disturbed by the events of the witch-hunt. Could it be that he is <u>suffering remorse</u> for what he has done? Or has he always been <u>unbalanced</u> and is simply unable to withstand the pressures of this troubled time? His later tears are shed over the loss of money, not of his niece.

It is clear that many changes have taken place since the end of Act 3. Cheever gives a description of Salem that shows the <u>devastation wrought upon the community</u> by the actions of Abigail and the court.

❝Vanished!❞

Abigail must have realised that it was only a matter of time before she was found to be a fraud. Why do you think Parris has waited for two days before telling the court that <u>Abigail has robbed him and has left Salem</u>?

<u>Abigail's flight has serious implications for Danforth</u>, who believed her claim that God was speaking through her. At the same time he is reminded of events at Andover, where a similar court has faced opposition from the townspeople and a rebellion against its authority. Consider his reaction to both pieces of news. What do we learn about his character and attitudes?

Reverend Parris makes a valid point: '<u>I fear there will be a riot here</u>'. The events at Andover, the flight of Abigail and Mercy, and the imminent execution of respected citizens form <u>a potentially explosive combination</u>. He realises that it is important for the court to obtain the confession of at least one worthy citizen if it is to retain any public credibility.

"Mr Parris, you are a brainless man!"

Explore

In the 1996 film version, Miller has included an extra scene in which Abigail visits John in prison. She offers him money, which he refuses, so he can bribe the guards to release him, and then run away with her.

Danforth seems unmoved by the news about Abigail. Perhaps he sees it as just one more example of Parris's stupidity. Abigail and the other girls are not mentioned again in the play. Despite the fact that the court in Salem owes its very existence to their accusations, <u>the girls seem irrelevant once the proceedings are in motion</u>. That Abigail's disappearance is not worth even a comment shows the court's fanaticism. The witch-hunt has taken on a momentum of its own.

A clue to Parris's mental state is shown by his reaction to the dagger thrown at his door: '<u>I dare not step outside at night!</u>' He sees the imminent hanging of Proctor in terms of a danger to his own life rather than punishment for Proctor.

"While I speak God's law, I will not crack its voice with whimpering"

Danforth believes that to pardon the condemned would only 'cast doubt upon the guilt of them that died till now'. Does his <u>pride</u> drive him to refuse to admit in public that his court has been unjust and its judgments wrong? Danforth's reference to the 'resolution of the statutes' shows once again how important <u>the letter of the law and its authority</u> was in this society. He also makes reference to the Bible, to confirm that he has a responsibility not to reprieve the accused from '<u>the perfection of their punishment</u>'.

"no man knows when the harlots' cry will end his life"

The evil that the witch-hunt has brought upon Salem is graphically evoked in this comment by Hale. <u>Society is being</u>

Text commentary

undermined. How does his reference to Abigail and her friends as 'harlots' compare with his earlier opinions about them?

Hale's sense of guilt is evident in his comment: '<u>There is blood on my head</u>.' He has severed his connections with the court and is determined to help the innocent. In trying to do so, he is forced to counsel men to lie, to confess to crimes of which they are innocent. He himself feels <u>doubly damned</u> for doing so. In a dramatic speech, he comments on what he was like when he first came to Salem, 'bringing gifts of high religion'.

cleave to no faith when faith brings blood

Elizabeth contemptuously rejects Hale's advice as the 'Devil's argument'. Remember that the last time Elizabeth felt compelled to lie, her husband was sent to prison because of it. She is not likely to make that same mistake twice. Although she and John are in desperate circumstances, <u>Elizabeth's sense of right and wrong remains steadfast</u>.

Danforth allows Elizabeth to see her husband alone, hoping that the sight of him will encourage her to persuade him to confess. <u>The love they show for each other transcends the squalor of their surroundings</u> and their desperate state.

more weight

Elizabeth's description of <u>Giles's death</u> tells us a great deal about him, as well as satisfying the audience's curiosity as to what became of him. Although he had faults, he had <u>great strength of character</u>. John is numbed by her description. If an old man can die in so heroic a manner, without lying or going against his conscience, how can Proctor reconcile himself to confessing in order to save his own life?

I cannot mount the gibbet like a saint

Rebecca's courageous stand in refusing to confess points out clearly the morally correct path John should follow. However, he is only too aware of <u>the discrepancy</u> <u>between</u> <u>her</u> <u>spotless</u> <u>life</u> <u>and</u> <u>his</u> <u>own</u> <u>tainted</u> <u>one</u>. He reasons that as he has already sinned, he is already damned. By the  end of Act 4, John has shrugged off this apathetic attitude. Try to track John's progress towards realising, at the end of the play, that he does have 'some shred of goodness'.

I would have your forgiveness, Elizabeth

Elizabeth wants John to live, but – in the same way that she feels it is not her place to advise him or to judge him – <u>she</u> <u>cannot</u> <u>forgive</u> <u>him</u>. She recognises, crucially, that he must forgive himself, for without this knowledge he can never again be at peace. At this moment, Elizabeth shows a deeper understanding of the situation than John. Her admission that '<u>It</u> <u>needs</u> <u>a</u> <u>cold</u> <u>wife</u> <u>to</u> <u>prompt</u> <u>lechery</u>' marks her own moment of truth. It takes great strength of character for her to <u>admit</u> <u>her</u> <u>contribution</u> <u>to</u> <u>her</u> <u>husband's</u> <u>adultery</u>. The reason that she gives for her coldness is that she regarded herself as too plain to keep a husband's love, so always suspected him. Elizabeth's honesty about her coldness perhaps makes it easier for John to make his own decision, for the next words he speaks, when Hathorne enters, are: 'I want my life'.

Explore

'It were a cold house I kept.' Look back to Act 2 and also to Abigail's judgement about Elizabeth's coldness to see what truth there is in this statement.

Then who will judge me?

There are two answers to John Proctor's question: God and John Proctor. Proctor recognises that a false confession would be a lie and therefore a sin. Coming to terms with this, ironically, helps him to find the strength to act according to his conscience later on.

In bringing <u>Rebecca Nurse</u> before John Proctor, Danforth makes errors of judgement. This brave old woman has no more intention of confessing or lying now than she did when she was first brought before the court. <u>Her courage in standing by her beliefs only strengthens John's resolve</u>. In attempting to persuade John to accuse Rebecca Nurse, Danforth makes it blindingly clear to John what the consequences of confession would be. It is not a course that a good man such as John would follow. The execution of Rebecca Nurse is the most potent sign of how absurd, as well as how evil, the persecution has become. On Hale's first entry in Act 1, he recognised her as looking exactly like '<u>such a good soul</u>' should; throughout the play you can find similar statements. Here in Act 4 her conduct and character have clearly not changed, but she is about to be executed.

There is <u>a sense of urgency</u> in this part of the play. The court officials are working against time – hangings were traditionally held at daybreak and there are repeated references to the sun rising. A signed confession from John Proctor would justify both the previous hangings and those which are proposed, and would be a great prize for Danforth: '<u>It will strike the village that Proctor confesses</u>'. He needs the confession nailed to the church door to reassert his authority and to prevent any possible uprising.

> ❝*How may I live without my name?*❞

John's will to live is strong, but his desire to keep his good name is stronger. It is not simply a matter of reputation; <u>his name is his identity</u>. If he publicly gives his name to this confession, he will no longer be recognisable to himself as 'John Proctor'. Danforth's ruthless insistence on a signed, truthful confession pushes John to do what he has for so long avoided – to follow his conscience. <u>He tears up his confession</u>.

Explore

What critical comment has John made in Act 2 about Elizabeth's heart? Why is 'a stony heart' seen as a good thing here?

This is reminiscent of Act 2 when he tore up Danforth's warrant for Elizabeth's arrest. On that occasion, he acted impulsively in anger and fear. Now, he is emotional and furious, but perfectly aware of his actions and sure that he is right. His final words: '<u>Show honour now, show a stony heart and sink them with it</u>', and his passionate kissing of Elizabeth, show his sureness and determination.

Hale, unlike Parris, has undergone a marked change during the course of the play. When he pleads with Elizabeth to persuade John to lie in order to save his life, he appears to have <u>lost sight of his religious duty to save souls, not bodies</u>. He misjudges John when he condemns his decision as stemming from 'pride' and 'vanity'. Perhaps Hale partly wants the confessions for selfish reasons, so that he no longer has blood on his conscience.

Explore

Look closely at the tone of Elizabeth's words at end the play. How do you think they should be said?

Compare the final scene and the opening scene of the play. Here, the sun pours in as in the first scene, but this time it perhaps carries a sense of <u>hope</u>. Hale 'weeps in frantic prayer'. Unlike Parris's prayer in the opening scene, does he perhaps pray not only for himself, but for John Proctor and Rebecca?

❝Echoes down the corridor❞

The ending of the play is conclusive only in terms of John Proctor's moral decision and the executions of himself and Rebecca. This is as it should be, as the play focuses on issues of conscience and is not a historical chronicle. <u>Many narrative strands are left hanging</u>. Is Abigail re-captured? Does Paris maintain his position as minister? Is there an uprising against the witch-trials? These are not essential parts of the drama, but for the reader of the text Arthur Miller adds a few answers in this section.

Explore

It would be useful for you to read Arthur Miller's essay, 'The Crucible in History'.

In his essay, 'The Crucible in History' (1999) Miller explains his motivation for writing the play, gives historical information and his views on the Salem incident and its parallels with the 'Red Hunt' of the 1950s. He is glad that he wrote *The Crucible*, but has often wished that he 'had the temperament to have done an absurd comedy, since that is what the situation often deserved'. He says in another essay, 'Clinton in Salem', that as a result of the witchcraft trials, '<u>Salem purified itself nearly to death, but in the end some good may have come of it</u>'.

Text commentary

A process of elimination

Delete two of the three alternatives given to find the correct plot.

1   Sarah Good and Tituba discuss the 'pleasureman' devil of England/Massachusetts/Barbados.

2   We hear how Hale is pleading/praying/arguing with the prisoners.

3   Abigail has run away with Mercy Lewis/Mary Warren/Ruth Putnam.

4   Six/twelve/thirty people have already been hanged.

5   Hale/Hathorne/Danforth urges Elizabeth to persuade her husband to confess.

6   Elizabeth describes how Rebecca/Goody Osburn/Giles died.

7   John's final words are to Danforth/Parris/Elizabeth.

8   The play ends on a scream/drumroll/woman's cry.

Who? What? Why? When? Where? How?

1   Whom has John Proctor attempted to strike?

2   What is it that John claims is keeping him from confessing?

3   What external evidence is there in Salem that things are going wrong?

4   Why does Giles refuse to confess?

5   How does John justify his decision to confess?

Who says ... ?

1   'You cannot hang this sort. There is danger for me. I dare not step outside at night.'

2   'Mr Parris, you are a brainless man.'

3   'I came into this village like a bridegroom to his beloved, bearing gifts of high religion'

4   'More weight.'

5   'Why, it is a lie, it is a lie; how may I damn myself? I cannot, I cannot.'

Take a moment to consider ...

What would the thoughts of Elizabeth Proctor be, after the ending of the play?

- To prepare for an exam, you should read the text in full at least twice, preferably three times. You need to know it very well.

- If your text is to be studied for an 'open book' exam, make sure that you take your book with you. However, you should not rely too much on the book – you haven't got time. If you are not allowed to take the text with you, you will need to memorise brief quotations.

- You need to decide fairly swiftly which question to answer. Choose a question which best allows you to demonstrate your understanding and personal ideas.

- Make sure you understand exactly what the question is asking you to do.

- **Plan** your answer (see page 76).

- Always have a short introduction giving an overview of the topic. Refer to your plan as you write to ensure you keep on task. Divide your ideas into paragraphs; without them you may not get above a D grade. Try to leave time for a brief conclusion.

- Remember, **Point–Quotation–Comment**: In Act 2 John Proctor has a strained relationship with his wife [**point**] who, he says, needs to 'learn charity' [**quotation**]. She is finding it difficult to come to terms with his affair with Abigail [**comment**].

- The key word in writing essays in exams is **timing**. You must know how long you have for each question and stick to this.

- Never forget that you are writing about a play that is meant to be performed, not just read, so consider the effect on the audience in your responses.

- Leave yourself a few minutes to check through your work. It does not look impressive if you misspell the names of characters, settings or the author himself.

- Timing is not so crucial for coursework essays, so this is your chance to show what you can really do without having to write under pressure.

- You can obviously go into far more detail than you are able to in an examination. You should aim for about 1000 words, but your teacher will advise you further.

- If you have a choice of title, make sure you select one that grabs your interest and gives you plenty of opportunity to develop your ideas.

- Plan your work (see page 76). Make sure that you often refer to the plan and the title as you write, to check that you are not drifting off course.

- Use quotations frequently but carefully, and try to introduce them smoothly. It is often effective to quote just one or two words.

- Try to state your own opinion, with phrases such as 'This suggests to me ...'. You will be credited for your ideas as long as you explain why you think them.

- Putting the play in context is very important. Include relevant background detail and explain how the cultural and historical setting affects the writer's choice of language.

- Make sure that you include a short conclusion by summing up your key ideas.

- Don't be tempted to copy large chunks of essays available on the Internet. Your teacher will immediately notice what you have done and will not reward it.

- It is a good idea, if possible, to word process your essay. This will enable you to make changes and improvements to your final draft more easily.

Writing essays

> **There is a murdering witch among us, bound to keep herself in the dark**

This unsettling statement from Act 1 shows Putnam's belief in the presence of witchcraft. It is convenient for him to believe in it, since his motivation is to acquire other people's land. The motif of darkness represents secrecy and evil.

> **I will bring a pointy reckoning that will shudder you**

Abigail's threat to the other girls at the start of the play shows her vindictiveness and power over others. The use of the adjective 'pointy' has ominous connotations of cruel vengeance. She speaks very directly – the more normal phrase would be 'will make you shudder'. Her violent language matches her violent actions to Betty.

> **Here is all the invisible world, caught, defined and calculated**

Hale, shortly after his arrival in Salem, refers to his weighty tomes on Demonology. He is so caught up in his learning that he fails to see that you cannot define something so abstract; this is later a problem in the witch trials. His carefully balanced sentence, with its list of three, gives it the quality of a rehearsed speech. Later, Hale comes to realise that the words are not true.

> **Let you look sometimes for the goodness in me, and judge me not**

John's words to Elizabeth in Act 2 show the idea of judgement that runs through the play, and also introduce the quality of goodness that becomes the key point in his character.

Notice how Miller creates speech patterns different from our own, by writing 'Let you look', to create a suggestion of seventeenth-century Puritan language.

> **"Now Hell and Heaven grapple on our backs and all our old pretence is ripped away"**

In John Proctor's dramatic speech at the end of Act 2, the graphic language with strong, active verbs shows the tremendous struggle the people have on their hands. 'Hell' has, unusually, been placed first in the phrase, indicating the fear that is uppermost in John's mind, for Hell now seems to have the strongest hold on Salem.

> **"We burn a hot fire here; it melts down all concealment"**

This line, from the trial in Act 3, strongly implies the 'Crucible' of the title. It also suggests hell fires, though Danforth means the fire of purification, and links with the motif of heat running through the text. What he says is not true, for his 'hot fire' simply encourages more people to lie and practise 'concealment'.

> **"I have given you my soul; leave me my name!"**

John's words at the climax of Act 4 link with the theme of identity. Giving away his soul – by which he means forsaking his personal integrity – would be the highest price to pay. He speaks with total passion and intensity. This is when John reaches a decision about his life, as his next action is to rip up his confession.

1. Explore how Miller creates a believable sense of the past in The Crucible.

2. Select an important character who you believe to be a villain. Analyse what makes that character villainous and how it adds to the play as a whole.

3. You are Deputy Governor Danforth. Write the arrest warrants of Elizabeth Proctor, Martha Corey and Rebecca Nurse, explaining why you believe they ought to stand trial.

4. 'Can one person make a difference?' Explore the extent to which The Crucible answers this question.

5. You are Elizabeth Proctor. Write a diary entry, from before your arrest, detailing your thoughts and fears about the relationship between your husband and Abigail.

6. You are a director. Discuss what advice you would give to the actors playing Abigail and Parris in the first scene.

7. Choose one of the key characters from the play and discuss how Miller helps the audience to engage with them to such an extent.

8. Miller explained that he saw witch-hunts as an 'inexplicable darkness' until he saw modern parallels. How far do you think Miller has been successful in creating a warning about such acts of 'darkness'?

9. Select an Act that you think is dramatically powerful and explain how Miller makes it so effective.

10. Explore the significance of the title of The Crucible and show how this is developed through the author's use of plot, character, imagery and language.

11. Explore the different settings of each Act, showing how Miller makes effective use of them.

12 Write three diary entries for Abigail, beginning with Betty being sick and ending when she runs away from Salem with Mercy Lewis. Be careful to use appropriate tone and language.

13 In what ways does Miller succeed in making the moment when John Proctor tears up the confession in Act 4 particularly dramatic?

14 How does Miller present the idea of persecution of the 'witches' in the play?

15 You are John Proctor the night before you are due to be hanged. Write a letter to Elizabeth explaining why you felt that you were right to act in the way you did.

16 Explore the ways in which Arthur Miller makes the ending of Act 1 especially dramatic. How does this compare to the tone and atmosphere at the start of the Act?

17 Examine the character of John Proctor, considering the ways in which Miller makes him a suitable protagonist for his own views on society and morality.

18 What makes the ending of Act 3 so dramatically intense? In your answer, you should look at the actions of the characters, the stage directions and any use of lighting or sound effects.

19 Choose two of the minor characters from the play. Discuss what you think they add to the plot and suggest why Miller chose to present them in the way that he did.

20 Explore the theme of evil in the play and consider the different ways in which it is presented.

21 Show how Miller presents two contrasting types of woman in Elizabeth Proctor and Abigail Williams. Explore your reaction to the characters at different points during the play.

Spidergrams for questions 5, 13 and 20 are shown on pages 77–79.

It is very important to be organised in your approach. Time spent in planning your response will be reflected in the grade you receive.

- The first thing to do is to read the question very carefully to make sure you fully understand it and then highlight key words.

- You will need to make some notes on the topic to help you. This can be done in various ways: a list; subheadings; spidergram; or a mind map.

- The advantage of using a spidergram, like those shown on the following pages, is that it lets you expand your ideas in a clearly linked, visual way. Put the essay title in the centre of the page. From this a number of key ideas will come out in the form of branches.

- By focusing on each key idea in turn, you will be able to branch out further, as your brain makes connections between the ideas.

- Since a spidergram is a way of charting your knowledge, it is also an excellent revision aid. You could work through a number of essay titles in this way.

- Some people prefer to make a spidergram even more visual, by colour coding ideas and adding pictures or symbols.

- In the planning stage of an essay it is also a good idea to jot down some useful quotations. These need not be lengthy and can be added to your spidergram.

- Each branch of a spidergram might form a separate paragraph in your essay. You can number the branches, so that you are clear about the order of your points. Deal with the main points first.

- Some students say that they do not like planning and that they never do so, but the majority of candidates do significantly better when they plan their answers.

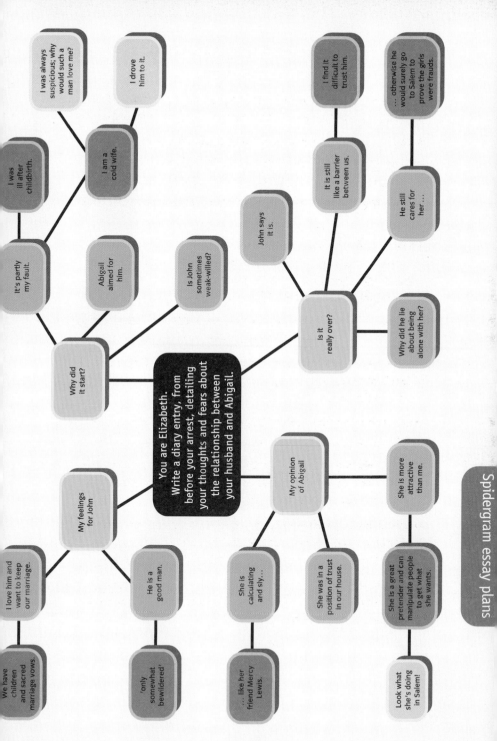

You are Elizabeth. Write a diary entry, from before your arrest, detailing your thoughts and fears about the relationship between your husband and Abigail.

Why did it start?
- I am a cold wife.
  - I was always suspicious; why would such a man love me?
  - I drove him to it.
- It's partly my fault.
  - I was ill after childbirth.
- Abigail aimed for him.
- Is John sometimes weak-willed?

Is it really over?
- John says it is.
  - It is still like a barrier between us.
  - I find it difficult to trust him.
- He still cares for her ...
  - ... otherwise he would surely go to Salem to prove the girls were frauds.
- Why did he lie about being alone with her?

My feelings for John
- I love him and want to keep our marriage.
- We have children and sacred marriage vows.
- He is a good man.
  - 'only somewhat bewildered'

My opinion of Abigail
- She is more attractive than me.
- She is calculating and sly, ...
  - ... like her friend Mercy Lewis.
- She was in a position of trust in our house.
- She is a great pretender and can manipulate people to get what she wants.
  - Look what she's doing in Salem!

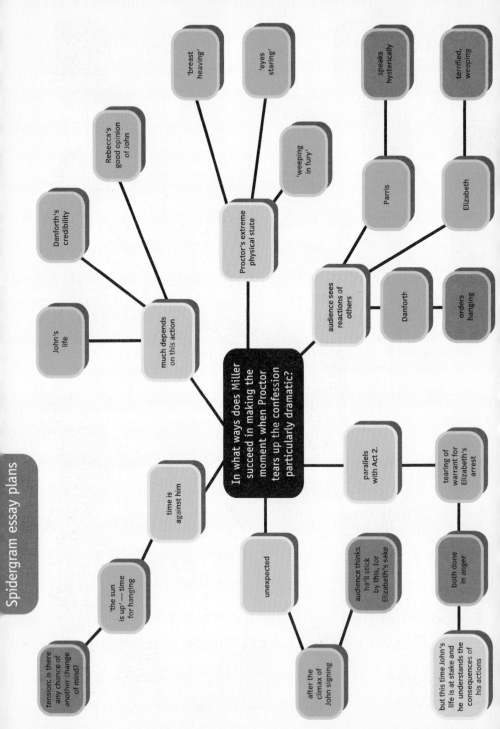

In what ways does Miller succeed in making the moment when Proctor tears up the confession particularly dramatic?

- much depends on this action
  - John's life
  - Danforth's credibility
  - Rebecca's good opinion of John
- Proctor's extreme physical state
  - 'breast heaving'
  - 'eyes staring'
  - 'weeping in fury'
- audience sees reactions of others
  - Parris
    - speaks hysterically
  - Elizabeth
    - terrified, weeping
  - Danforth
    - orders hanging
- parallels with Act 2.
  - tearing of warrant for Elizabeth's arrest
    - both done in anger
    - but this time John's life is at stake and he understands the consequences of his actions
- unexpected
  - after the climax of John signing
  - audience thinks he'll stick by this, for Elizabeth's sake
- time is against him
  - 'the sun is up' — time for hanging
    - tension: is there any chance of another change of mind?

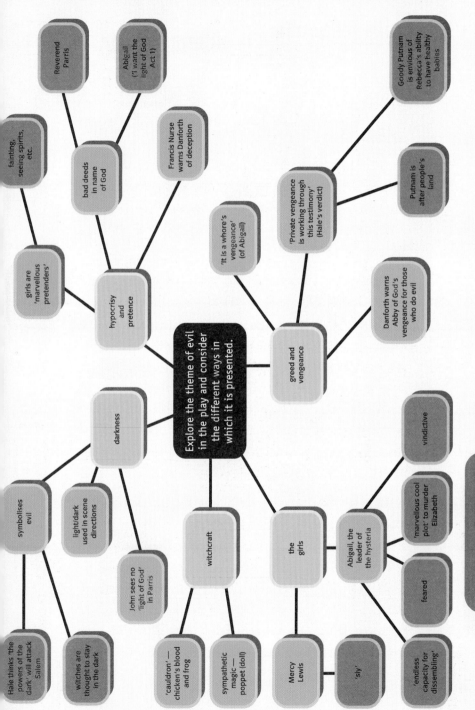

Explore the theme of evil in the play and consider the different ways in which it is presented.

hypocrisy and pretence
- Reverend Parris
- Abigail ('I want the light of God Act 1)
- fainting, seeing spirits, etc.
- girls are 'marvellous pretenders'
- bad deeds in name of God
- Francis Nurse warns Danforth of deception

greed and vengeance
- 'It is a whore's vengeance' (of Abigail)
- 'Private vengeance is working through this testimony' (Hale's verdict)
- Goody Putnam is envious of Rebecca's ability to have healthy babies
- Putnam is after people's land
- Danforth warns Abby of God's vengeance for those who do evil

darkness
- symbolises evil
- light/dark used in scene directions
- Hale thinks 'the powers of the dark' will attack Salem
- witches are thought to stay in the dark
- John sees no 'light of God' in Parris

witchcraft
- 'cauldron' — chicken's blood and frog
- sympathetic magic — poppet (doll)

the girls
- Mercy Lewis
- 'sly'
- Abigail, the leader of the hysteria
  - vindictive
  - 'marvellous cool plot' to murder Elizabeth
  - feared
  - 'endless capacity for dissembling'

Sample response

Explore the ways in which Arthur Miller makes the ending to Act 1 so dramatic (from Abigail's words 'I never sold myself' to the end of the scene).

This extract begins when Abigail is forced to explain herself in front of Parris and Hale. You can tell she is quite desperate because her first words are all exclamations, which would show that she is maybe shouting so that Hale believes her. ✔ She says: 'I'm a good girl' and 'I'm a proper girl.'

At this stage Mrs Putnam enters with Tituba and Abigail points at her to show that she is to blame. She says that Tituba made her do it and Tituba is 'shocked and angry'. I think she is shocked because she thought Abby would stay loyal to her, but instead she has no problems with placing the blame on someone else. Arthur Miller draws attention to the witchcraft accusation by repetition of the word 'blood'. Abby tells Parris that Tituba made her 'drink blood' and Parris replies, 'Blood!' By including these details, it makes the activities seem very evil, especially when Mrs Putnam asks if it was her 'baby's blood'. ✔✔

Abigail is very clever in this scene because she then takes the opportunity to also blame Tituba for other 'crimes' she has been accused of, such as giggling in church and wandering around with no clothes on. Tituba tries to defend herself but she is not really given a chance to speak. ✔ Eventually, Putnam and Parris make Tituba so frightened of being whipped or hanged that she makes a 'confession'. In the stage directions it says Tituba is 'terrified' and she 'falls to her knees' – this emphasises how scared she is. ✔

Putnam sees how frightened she is and plants the idea that Sarah Good might be one of the Devil's witches. Tituba is desperate not to be hanged and understands that if she blames someone else, she will be let off. Significantly, the first names she mentions are 'Goody Good' and 'Goody Osburn'. Mrs Putnam seizes on this piece of information: 'I knew it! Goody Osburn were midwife to me three times'.

The scene becomes even more dramatic when Abigail suddenly 'rises, staring as though inspired'. ✓ She tells Hale she wishes to 'open' herself, which means she wants to confess. This shows how clever she is, because she sees that this is her chance to move the blame from herself onto someone else. She then lists several women who she has supposedly seen with the devil. ✓

When the unmoving Betty suddenly leaps up and begins chanting it is even more dramatic because it seems as if the confessing has made Betty well again. There is lots of repetition as the two girls shout out names and in the middle of the chaos Parris begins shouting a prayer. ✓ The curtain falls in the middle of the action leaving the audience wanting to know what happens. ✓

Examiner's comments

This is a very sound response with good understanding of the stagecraft present in this scene and how the action becomes more dramatic. Quotations are well chosen and support points made. There is a slight tendency to narrate the story, but the essay is well structured and very competent. Good appreciation of how the author's use of language creates dramatic effect is shown. This is a high level C answer.

Sample response

Explore the ways in which Arthur Miller makes the ending to Act 1
so dramatic (from Abigail's words 'I never sold myself 'to the end
of the scene).

The extract begins with Abigail explaining her doubtful actions in
front of Parris, Putnam and Hale. She has changed from her earlier
confident attitude and seems desperate. Her first sentences are all
exclamations, indicating her increasing need to be believed. ✓
She shouts 'I'm a proper girl', appealing to the Puritan sense of the
term. She means that she lives her life according to strict, religious
rules, which we know is not true.

Abigail seizes the opportunity of Tituba's entrance and points at
her, indicating that she is to blame. This action visually reinforces
her words. ✓ The stage directions say that Tituba is 'shocked
and angry', probably because she mistakenly believed Abby would
remain loyal to her. Instead, the manipulative Abby has no
problems laying the blame on someone else. ✓ The repetition of
the word 'blood' emphasises the evil nature of witchcraft, and
Abby's revelation that the girls had been drinking blood graphically
illustrates that their nocturnal activities were not as harmless as we
had first been led to believe, especially when Mrs Putnam asks if it
was her 'baby's blood'. ✓✓

Abigail reveals her manipulative nature when she takes the chance
to blame Tituba for other examples of her wilful and wanton
behaviour – giggling in church and standing naked at night
(presumably waiting to tempt John Proctor). ✓ Tituba tries to

defend herself but she is not really given a chance to speak. Hale is not interested in hearing her defence, only hearing about her satanic influence. ✓ Putnam and Parris use very clever tactics to extract Tituba's confession – threatening her with being whipped or hanged. The stage directions reveal she is 'terrified' and she 'falls to her knees'. This action would clearly reveal how frightened she is, but more importantly would serve to show the audience how subservient she is, and totally at the mercy of Hale and Putnam. From the audience's point of view it looks as though she is begging for her life. ✓✓

When Putnam, taking advantage of the situation, plants the name of Sarah Good in her thoughts, Tituba is so desperate not to be hanged that she sees a false confession as a way out and, like Abigail, chooses to blame someone else. ✓ Significantly, the first name she mentions is that of Goody Good, before also accusing Sarah Osburn, the midwife. Mrs Putnam seizes the chance to seek 'pointy reckoning' for her babies' deaths by dramatically shouting: 'I knew it!' ✓

The sense of drama increases when Abigail, who has been silent during Tituba's interrogation, suddenly 'rises, staring as though inspired'. Miller gives precise lighting instructions here, that she is to be bathed in an almost heavenly light, which would make her transformation extremely dramatic on stage. ✓✓ She declares a desire to 'open' herself, which shows how clever she is. Once again she takes the opportunity to shift the blame onto someone else.

When the comatose Betty suddenly springs to life and begins a distinctly witch-like chant, the action becomes even more dramatically powerful. The effect is that confessing has somehow made Betty well. ✓ In the midst of the girls' rhythmic chanting and the ensuing chaos, Parris begins shouting a prayer of thanksgiving. It is interesting that on this occasion the holy words leave Betty unaffected, unlike earlier in the scene – surely clear evidence to suggest the girls' lack of sincerity. ✓✓

The Act ends with a series of repeated, single lines – 'I saw Alice Barrow with the devil' – each one condemning yet another innocent woman. Miller's final dramatic device is to have the curtain fall while the girls are still shouting names. This leaves the audience in shock and very suddenly ends the momentum and tension built up in the final stages of the Act, which is, in many ways, simply a precursor to the drama of Act 3. ✓

Examiner's comments

This is a perceptive and thoughtful response, which reveals thorough understanding of what makes the scene dramatic. The candidate considers plot, character and elements of stagecraft to make points, all of which are supported by quotations from the text. This is a confident and assured answer, which is well structured and accurate.

Quick quiz answers

Quick quiz 1

A process of elimination

1   The play is set in 1692.
2   Reverend Parris is praying by his daughter's bed.
3   Abigail warns the other girls to say nothing.
4   John Proctor has slept with Abigail.
5   Only Rebecca can calm Betty.
6   Abigail accuses Tituba of being a witch.

Who? What? Why? When? Where? How?

1   Reverend Parris
2   farmer
3   They were killed by American Indians.
4   Hale carries a pile of heavy books, which he refers to 'with a tasty love of intellectual pursuit'.

Who is this?

1   Mary Warren
2   Abigail Williams
3   Mercy Lewis
4   Ruth Putnam (described by Mrs Putnam)
5   Tituba (described by Parris)

Take a moment to consider …
An overture is an opening (usually to a piece of music). This Act is an introduction, which sets everything in motion and paves the way for the horrors to come. Music is important to Miller, and there are certain musical qualities in the Act, for example in the stylised, rhythmical language and the different character groupings on stage.

Quick quiz 2

A process of elimination

1   Act 2 is set in the Proctors' house.
2   It is eight days after the last Act.
3   Fourteen people are already in jail.
4   Hale arrives at the house.
5   John forgets the Commandment concerning adultery.
6   John is determined to force Mary to give evidence against Abigail.

Who? What? Why? When? Where? How?

1   Hale (because he understands his betrayal of Elizabeth but does nothing).
2   Cheever
3   a 'poppet' or rag doll she has made
4   'for the marvellous and supernatural murder of Goody Putnam's babies'
5   She shouts that she has saved Elizabeth's life.
6   She sees Mary stick a needle in the poppet that is to be a present for Elizabeth and, at dinner, sticks a pin in her own stomach, claiming that Elizabeth's spirit pushed it in.

Who says … ?

1   Elizabeth (to John)
2   Hale (to John)
3   Elizabeth (to John)

Take a moment to consider …
It is the only Act set away from Salem. It is also the only one not in

any sort of official building. The setting of Act 1, although it is the Reverend Parris's home, seems to be a meeting place for the community; Act 3 is in the court room and Act 4 in the jail.

Quick quiz 3
A process of elimination

1 Proctor brings Mary to testify against the girls.
2 Danforth offers to let the pregnant Elizabeth live for a year.
3 John gives the judges a testament with 91 signatures.
4 Danforth orders all these people to be arrested for questioning.
5 Elizabeth denies that John is a lecher in order to save his good name.
6 Mary, attacked on all fronts, accuses John Proctor.
7 John and Giles are arrested.
8 Hale denounces the proceedings.

Who? What? Why? When? Where? How?

1 Abigail
2 Abigail (according to John)
3 a 'yellow bird' – Mary in a witch form
4 'In the proper place – where my beasts are bedded'.
5 'The vestry room of the Salem meeting house, now serving as the anteroom of the General Court.'

Who says ... ?

1 Danforth
2 John, in anguish, at the end of the Act

3 John quotes the angel Raphael's words to bolster up Mary's courage
4 Mary, at the end of the Act, when she turns against John

Take a moment to consider ...
John's 'heat' is partly sexual (there are tangible sparks between him and Abigail), and partly a different kind of passion, which finds occasional release in anger and violence. He threatens to whip Mary in Act 2, tears up his wife's warrant, grabs Abigail by the hair in this Act and rails against his fate.

Quick quiz 4
A process of elimination

1 Sarah Good and Tituba discuss the 'pleasureman' devil of Barbados.
2 We hear how Hale is praying with the prisoners.
3 Abigail has run away with Mercy Lewis.
4 Twelve people have already been hanged.
5 Hale urges Elizabeth to persuade her husband to confess.
6 Elizabeth describes how Giles died.
7 John's final words are to Elizabeth.
8 The play ends on a drumroll.

Who? What? Why? When? Where? How?

1 Herrick, the marshal
2 'Spite only keeps me silent.'
3 Hale: 'there are orphans wandering from house to house;

abandoned cattle bellow on the highroads, the stink of rotting crops hangs everywhere'

4   If Giles confessed his property would have been confiscated; by remaining silent his sons will inherit his farm.

5   He would be a fraud to die like a saint.

Who says …?

1   Parris
2   Danforth
3   Hale
4   Giles (to his tormentors)
5   Rebecca, refusing to 'confess'

Take a moment to consider …
You may well receive an empathy task like this. Elizabeth will have a mixture of emotions. Obviously she will be grief-stricken – we know she is almost collapsing at the end – and will also be worried, for she is left with the farm to run and a young family to raise and is pregnant again. She will be full of admiration for John, that he showed integrity at the end and has shown real 'goodness'. She may regret the difficulties they had in their marriage, including her contribution to them.

Page 12, Arthur Miller, © Hellestad Rune/Corbis Sygma
Page 15, Scene, © Robbie Jack/Corbis

First published 1994
Revised edition 2004

Letts Educational
Chiswick Centre
414 Chiswick High Road
London W4 5TF
Tel: 020 8996 3333

Text © John Mahoney and Stewart Martin 1994
2004 edition revised by Claire Crane and Juliet Walker

Cover and text design by Hardlines Ltd., Charlbury, Oxfordshire.

Typeset by Letterpart Ltd., Reigate, Surrey.

Graphic illustration by Beehive Illustration, Cirencester, Gloucestershire.

Commissioned by Cassandra Birmingham

Editorial project management by Vicky Butt

Printed in Italy.

Design and illustration © Letts Educational Ltd

British Library Cataloguing in Publication Data. A CIP record of this book is available from the British Library.

ISBN 1 84315 320 3

Letts Educational is a division of Granada Learning, part of Granada plc.